New Designs

An Anthology
of Spiritual Vision,

Joan D. Chittister, OSB

Benetvision

ISBN: 1-890890-13-8

02 03 04 05 06 5 4 3 2 1

Benetvision
355 East Ninth Street
Erie, Pennsylvania 16503-1107

814-459-5994
benetvision@eriebenedictines.org
www.eriebenedictines.org

Table of Contents

Discipleship

*Discipleship for a Priestly People
in a Priestless Period*

Two stories may explain these reflections on discipleship in an interim age best. The first insight is from the poet Basho who wrote: "I do not seek to follow in the footsteps of those of old. I seek the things they sought."

And the second story is from ancient monastic literature: Once upon a time, the story goes, a teacher traveled with great difficulty to a far away monastery because there was an old monastic there who had a reputation for asking very piercing spiritual questions. "Holy One," the teacher said. "Give me a question that will renew my soul." "Ah, yes, then," the old monastic said, "your question is, What do they need?"

The teacher wrestled with the question for days but then, depressed, gave up and went back to the old monastic in disgust. "Holy One," the teacher said, "I came here because I'm tired and depressed and dry. I didn't come here to talk about my ministry. I came here to talk about my spiritual life. Please give me another question." "Ah, well, of course. Now I see," the old monastic said, "in that case, the right question for you is not, What do they need? The right question for you is, What do they really need?"

9

The question haunts me. What do the people really need in a period when the sacraments are being lost in a sacramental church but all approaches to the question—even the consciousness that there is a question to be asked conscientiously about the nature and meaning of priesthood—is being blocked, obstructed, denied, and suppressed?

"What do they really need?" becomes a haunting refrain in me for more reasons than the philosophical. Up at the top of a Mexican mountain, beyond miles of rutted road and wet, flowing clay, I toured an Indian village that was visited by a priest only once a year. But that was years ago. Now the mountain is just as high and the priest is fifteen years older.

Five years ago I spoke in an American parish of 6,000 families—one of those new western phenomena known as "mega-churches" that is served by three priests. There is no priest shortage there however, the priests want you to know, because the bishop has redefined the optimum ratio of priest to people from one to every 250 families to one priest to every 2,000 families. In diocese after diocese parishes are being merged, closed, turned into sacramental way stations served by retired priests or married male deacons, both of which are designed to keep the church male, whether it is ministering or not. The number of priests is declining. The number of Catholics is increasing, the number of lay ministers being certified is rising in every academic system despite the fact that their services are being restricted, rejected or made redundant in parish after parish.

And in the United States, there's a five-year-old girl who, when her parents answered her question about the absence of women priests in their parish with the flat explanation that "We don't have girl-priests in our church," thought for a minute and then responded sharply, "Then why do we go there?"!

Clearly, the church is changing even while it reasserts its changelessness.

It is a far cry from the dynamism of the early church in which Prisca and Lydia and Thecla and Phoebe and hundreds of women like them opened house churches, walked as disciples of Paul, "constrained him," the scripture says, to serve a given region, instructed people in the faith and ministered to the fledgling Christian communities with no apology, no argument, no tricky theological shell games about whether they were ministering *in persona Christi* or *in nomine Christi*.

Clearly, both the question and the answer are clear: What do they really need? They need what they needed when the temple became more important than the Torah; they need what they needed when the faith was more a vision than an institution. They need what they have always needed: They need Christian community, not patriarchal clericalism. They need the sacred, not the sexist. The people need more prophets, not more priests. They need discipleship, not canonical decrees.

So what is to be done at a time like this when what is sought and what is possible are two different things? To what are we to give our energy when we are told no energy is wanted? The questions may sound new but the answer is an old one, an ancient one, a true one. The answer is discipleship.

The temptation is to become weary in the apparently fruitless search for office. The call is to become recommitted to the essential, the ancient, the authentic demands of discipleship. But Christian discipleship is a very dangerous thing. It has put every person who ever accepted it at risk. It made every follower who ever took it seriously on alert for rejection, from Martin of Tours to John Henry Newman, from Mary Ward to Dorothy Day.

Discipleship cast every fragile new Christian community in tension with the times in which it grew. To be a Christian community meant to defy Roman imperialism, to stretch Judaism, to counter pagan values with Christian ones. It demanded very concrete presence; it took great courage, unending fortitude and clear public posture.

Real discipleship meant the rejection of emperor worship, the foreswearing of animal sacrifice, the inclusion of Gentiles, the elimination of dietary laws, the disavowal of circumcision, the acceptance of women and the supplanting of law with love, of nationalism with universalism. Then, the following of Christ was not an excursion into the intellectual, the philosophical, the airy-fairy. It was not an arm-wrestling match with a tradition that was more history warped by culture than it was the spirit free of the system. It was real and immediate and cosmic.

The problem with Christian discipleship is that instead of simply requiring a kind of academic or ascetic exercise—the implication of most kinds of discipleship—Christian discipleship requires a kind of living that is sure, eventually, to tumble a person from the banquet tables of prestigious boards and the reviewing stands of presidents, and the processions of ecclesiastical knighthood to the most suspect margins of both church and society.

To follow Jesus, in other words, is to follow the one who turns the world upside down, even the religious world. It is a tipsy arrangement at the very least. People with high need for approval, social status, and public respectability need not apply. "Following Jesus" is a circuitous route that leads always and everywhere to places where a "nice" person would not go, to moments of integrity we would so much rather do without.

The Christian carries a worldview that cries for fulfillment now. Christian discipleship is not preparation for the hereafter or an ecstatic distance from the present. Christian discipleship is the commitment to live a certain way now. To follow Christ is to set about fashioning a world where the standards into which we have been formed become the standards, we too often find, we must ultimately foreswear. Flag and fatherland, profit and power, chauvinism and sexism, clericalism and authoritarianism done in the name of Christ are not Christian virtues, whatever the system that looks to them for legitimacy.

Christian discipleship is about living in this world the way that Christ lived in his—touching lepers, raising donkeys from ditches on Sabbath days, questioning the unquestionable and consorting with women.

Discipleship implies a commitment to leave nets and homes, positions and securities, lordship and legalities to be now, in our own world, what Christ was for his: healer and prophet, voice and heart, call and sign of the God whose design for this world is justice and love. The disciple hears the poor, and ministers to the Hagars of this world who, having been used up by the establishment, are then abandoned to find their way alone, unaccompanied through a patriarchal world, unnoticed in a patriarchal world, unwanted in a patriarchal world but mightily, mightily patronized in a patriarchal world.

Discipleship is prepared to fly in the face of a world bent only on maintaining its own ends whatever the cost. The price is a high one. Teresa of Avila, John of the Cross and Joan of Arc were persecuted for opposing the hierarchy itself—and then, later, canonized. Discipleship cost Mary Ward her health, her reputation, and even a Catholic burial. Discipleship cost Martin Luther King, Jr. his life.

To the real disciple, to the true disciple the problem is clear: The church must not only preach the gospel, but it must not obstruct it. It must be what it says. It must demonstrate what it teaches. It must be judged by its own standards. Religion that colludes with the dispossession of the poor or the enslavement of the other in the name of patriotism becomes just one more instrument of the state. Religion that blesses oppressive governments in the name of obedience to an authority that denies the authority of conscience, makes itself an oppressor as well. Religion that goes mute in the face of massive militarization practiced in the name of national defense abandons the God of love for the preservation of the civil religion. Religion that preaches the equality of women but does nothing to demonstrate it within its own structures, that proclaims an ontology of equality but insists on an ecclesiology of superiority is out of sync with its best self and dangerously close to repeating the theological errors that underlie centuries of church sanctioned slavery.

The pauperization of women in the name of the sanctity and essentialism of motherhood flies in the face of the Jesus who overturned tables in the temple, contended with Pilate in the palace, chastised Peter to put away his sword and, despite the teaching of the day, cured the woman with the issue of blood and refused to allow his own apostles to silence the Samaritan woman on whose account, scripture tells us, "thousands believed that day."

Indeed, Jesus shows us, when women lack jurisdiction, church commissions lack women and even altar girls are barred in a Christian community that says they are permitted, the invisibility of women in the church threatens the very nature of the church.

Obviously discipleship is not based on sexism, on civil quietism or on private piety. On the contrary, discipleship confounds the "right reason" and "good sense" of patriarchy with right relationships and good heart. It pits the holy against the human. It pits the heart of Christ against the heartlessness of an eminently male-oriented, male-defined, male-controlled world. To be a disciple in the model of Judith and Esther, of Deborah and Ruth, of Mary and Mary Magdalene means to find ourselves forgers of a world where the weak confound the strong.

The disciple begins like the prophet Ruth to seek a world where the rich and the poor change places. The disciple sets out like the judge Deborah to shape a world where the last are made first and the first are last, starting with themselves. The disciple insists, as Jesus did, as the commander Judith did, on a world where women do what heretofore has been acceptable only for men simply because men said so. To the disciple who follows in the shadow of Esther, the savior of her people, the reign of God—the welcome of the outcast, the reverence of the other, the respect for creation—becomes a foreign land made home. "Come follow me" becomes an anthem of public proclamation from which no one, no one, is excluded and for which no risk is too great.

Discipleship, we know from the life of the Christ whom we follow, is not membership in a clerical social club called a church. That is not an ordination that the truly ordained can abide. Discipleship is not an intellectual exercise of assent to a body of doctrine. Discipleship is an attitude of mind, a quality of soul, a way of living that is not political but which has serious political implications, that may not be officially ecclesiastical but which changes the church that is more ecclesiastical than communal. Discipleship changes things because it simply cannot ignore things as they are, it refuses anything and everything that defies the will of God for humanity, no matter how sensible, no matter how reasonable, no matter how common, no matter how obvious, no matter how historically patriarchal, no matter how often it has been called "the will of God" by those who purport to determine what that is.

The disciple takes public issue with the values of a world that advantages only those who are already advantaged. The disciple takes aim at institutions that call themselves "freeing" but which keep half the people of the world in bondage, they take umbrage at systems that are more bent on keeping "those kind of people"—improper people, that is—out of them than they are in welcoming all people into them.

True discipleship takes the side always, always, always of the poor despite the power of the rich—not because the poor are more virtuous than the rich but because the God of love wills for them what the rich ignore for them. Discipleship cuts a reckless path through corporation types like Herod, through institution types like the Pharisees, through system types like the money-changers and through chauvinist types like apostles who want to send women away.

Discipleship stands bare naked in the middle of the world's marketplace and, in the name of Jesus, cries aloud all the cries of the world until someone, somewhere hears and responds to the poorest of the poor, the lowest of the low, the most outcast of the rejected. Anything else—all the pomp, all the gold lace and red silk, all the rituals in the world—the gospels attest, is certainly mediocre and surely bogus discipleship.

It is one thing, then, for an individual to summon the courage it takes to stand alone in the eye of a storm called "the real world." It is another thing entirely to see the church itself be anything less than the living Christ. Why? Because the church of Jesus Christ is not called to priesthood, the church of Christ is called to discipleship.

To see a church of Christ deny the poor and the outcast their due, institute the very systems in itself that it despises in society, is to see no church at all. It is at best religion reduced to one more social institution designed to comfort the comfortable but not to challenge the chains that bind most of humanity—all of its women—to the cross. In this kind of church, the gospel has been long reduced to the catechism. In this kind of church, prophecy dies and justice whimpers and the truth becomes too dim for the searching to see. Today, as never before in history, perhaps, the world and therefore the church within it, is being stretched to the breaking point by life situations that, if for no other reason than their immensity, are shaking the globe at its foundations.

New life questions emerge with startling impact and relentless persistence. And the greatest of them all is the woman's question. Women are most of the poor, most of the refugees, most of the uneducated, most of the beaten, most of the rejected of the world. In the church, educated, dedicated, committed women are ignored even in the pronouns of the Mass. Where is the presence of Jesus to the homeless woman, to the beggar woman, to the abandoned woman, to the woman alone, to the woman whose questions, cries and life experience have no place in the systems of the world and no place in the church either? Except, of course, to be defined as a second kind of human nature, not quite as competent, not quite as valued, not quite as human, not quite as graced by God as men?

What does the theology of discipleship demand here? What does the theology of a priestly people imply here? Are women simply half a disciple of Christ? To be half commissioned, half noticed, and half valued?

In the light of these situations, there are, consequently, questions in the Christian community today that cannot be massaged by footnotes nor obscured by jargon nor made palatable by the retreat to "faith." On the contrary, before these issues, the footnotes falter, the language serves only to heighten the question, faith itself demands the question. The discipleship of women is the question that is not going to go away. Indeed, the discipleship of the church in regard to women is the question that will, in the long run, prove the church itself.

In the woman's question the church is facing one of its most serious challenges to discipleship since the emergence of the slavery question when we argued, too, that slavery was the will of God. The major question facing Christians today, perhaps, is, What does discipleship mean in a church that doesn't want women? If discipleship is reduced to maleness, what does that do to the rest of the Christian dispensation? If only men can really live discipleship to the fullest, what is the use of a woman aspiring to discipleship at all? What does it mean for the women themselves who are faced with rejection, devaluation and a debatable theology based on the remnants of a bad biology theologized? What do we do when a church proclaims the equality of women but builds itself on structures that assure their inequality?

What, as well, does the rejection of women at the highest levels of the church mean for men who claim to be enlightened but continue to support the very system that mocks half the human race? What does it mean for the church that claims to be a follower of the Jesus who pulled asses out of ditches on the Sabbath and raised women from the dead and contended with the teachers of the faith—*mandatum* or no *mandatum*, definitive documents or no definitive documents? And finally what does it mean for a society badly in need of a cosmic worldview on the morning of a global age?

The answers are discouragingly clear on all counts. Christian discipleship is not simply in danger of being stunted. Discipleship has, in fact, become the enemy. Who we do not want to admit to full, official, legitimated discipleship—something the church itself teaches is required of us all—has become at least as problematic for the integrity of the church as the people who continue to exclude women from the offices of the church that shape its theology and minister to its people.

Women are beginning to wonder if discipleship has anything to do with them at all. And therein lies the contemporary question of discipleship. Some consider faithfulness to the gospel to mean doing what we have always done. Others find faithfulness only in being what we have always been. The distinction is crucial. The distinction is also essential to the understanding of discipleship in the modern church. When "the tradition" becomes synonymous with "the system" and maintaining the system becomes more important than maintaining the spirit of the tradition, discipleship shrivels and becomes at best "obedience" or "fidelity" to the past but not deep-down commitment to the presence of the living Christ confronting the leprosies of the age.

Discipleship presumes from each of us, from the church itself, that same kind of reckless, open, receiving, giving love that Jesus brought to the blind on the roads of Galilee, to the body of a dead girl, to the plea of the woman with the issue of blood.

Society called the blind sinful, a female child useless, a menstruating woman unclean, all of them marginal to the system, condemned to the fringes of life, excluded from the center of the synagogue, barred from the heart of the temple. But Jesus takes each of them to himself, despite the laws, regardless of the culture, notwithstanding the disapproval of the spiritual notables of the area and fills them with himself and sends them as himself out to the highways and byways of the entire world.

To be disciples of Jesus means that we must do the same. There are some things, it seems, that brook no rationalizing for the sake of institutional niceties. Discipleship infers, implies, requires no less than the confirming, ordaining, love of Jesus for everyone, everywhere regardless of who would dare to take upon themselves the audacious right to draw limits around the love of God. Discipleship and faith are of a piece. To say that we believe that God loves the poor, judges in their behalf, wills their deliverance but do nothing ourselves to free the poor, to hear their pleas, to lift their burdens, to act in their behalf, is an empty faith indeed. To say that God is love and not ourselves love as God loves may well be church but it is not Christianity.

To proclaim a theology of equality, to say that all persons are equal in God's sight and at the same time to maintain a theology of inequality, a spirituality of domination in the name of God that says that women have no place in the dominion of the church and the development of doctrine is to live a lie.

But if discipleship is the following of Jesus, beyond all bounds, at all costs, for the bringing of the reign of God, for the establishment of right relationships, then to ground a woman's calling to follow Christ in her ability to look like Jesus obstructs the very thing the church is founded to do. It obstructs a woman's ability to follow Christ to the full, to give her life for the others, to bless and preach and sacrifice and build community "in His name"—as the documents on priesthood say that a priestly people must. And it does it for the sake of religion and in defiance of the gospel itself. How can a church such as this call convincingly to the world in the name of justice to practice a justice it does not practice itself?

How is it that the church can call other institutions to deal with women as full human beings made in the image of God when their humanity is precisely what the church itself holds against them in the name of God? It is a philosophical question of immense proportions. It is the question which, like slavery, brings the church to the test. For the church to be present to the woman's question, to minister to it, to be disciple to it, the church must itself become converted to the issue. In fact, the church must become converted by the issue.

Men who do not take the woman's issue seriously may be priests but they cannot possibly be disciples. They cannot possibly be other Christs, not the Christ born of a woman. Not the Christ who commissioned women to preach him. Not the Christ who took faculties from a woman at Cana. Not the Christ who sent women to preach resurrection to apostles who would not believe it. Not the Christ who sent the Holy Spirit on Mary the woman as well as on Peter the man. Not the Christ who announced his messiahship as clearly to the Samaritan woman as to the Rock that shattered. If this is the Jesus whom we as Christians, as church, are to follow, then the discipleship of the church is now mightily in question.

Indeed, the poet Basho writes: "I do not seek to follow in the footsteps of those of old. I seek the things they sought."

Discipleship depends on our bringing the will of God for humankind to the questions of this age as Jesus did to his. As long as tradition is used to mean following in the footsteps of our past rather than seeking to maintain the spirit of the Christ in the present, then it is unlikely that we will preserve more than the shell of the church. The consciousness of the universalism of humanity across differences has become the thread that binds the world together in a global age. What was once a hierarchy of humankind is coming to be seen for what it is: the oppression of humankind.

To most of the world, the colonization of women is as unacceptable now as the colonial oppression of Africa, the crusades against Turks, the enslavement of blacks and the decimation of Indians in the name of God. In Asia, Buddhist women are demanding ordination and the right to make the sacred mandalas. In India, women are beginning to do the sacred dances and light the sacred fires. In Judaism, women study Torah and carry the scrolls and read the scriptures and lead the congregations. Only in the most backward, most legalistic, most primitive of cultures are women made invisible, made useless, made less than fully human, less than fully spiritual.

The humanization of the human race is upon us. The only question for the church is whether the humanization of the human race will lead as well to the Christianization of the Christian church. Otherwise, discipleship will die and the integrity of the church with it.

We must take discipleship seriously or we shall leave the church of the future with functionaries but without disciples. The fact is that Christianity lives in Christians, not in books, not in documents called "definitive" to hide the fact that they are at best time-bound. Not in platitudes about "special vocations," not in old errors dignified as "tradition."

The new fact of life is that discipleship to women and the discipleship of women are key to the discipleship of the rest of the church. The questions are clear. The answer is obscure and uncertain but crucial to the future of a church that claims to be eternal.

A priestly people in a priestless period must keep the total vision clearly in mind. But we must also keep the tasks of the present clearly in hand, and the task of the present is not preparation for ordination in a church that either doubts, or fears, the power of the truth to persuade and so denies the right to discuss the festering question of whether or not women can participate in the sacrament of orders. That would be premature, at best, if not downright damaging.

No, the task of the present in a time such as this is to use every organization to which we belong to develop the theology of the church to a point of critical mass.

We need a group free of *mandatums* that will organize seminars, hold public debates in the style of the great medieval disputations on the full humanity of Indians, hold teach-ins, sponsor publications, write books, post web sites and gather discussion groups around the topics of the infallibility of infallibility and the *sensus fidelium*.

The task of the present is surely for groups like this to question the clear exclusion of women from the restoration of the permanent diaconate, an official manner of discipleship that has theology, history, ritual, liturgy and tradition, firmly, fully and clearly on its side. It's time to bring into the light of day the discussions that lurk behind every church door, in every seeking heart.

If as Vatican II says, priesthood requires preaching, sacrifice and community building, then the preaching, shaping, and vision of a new notion of priest and deacon—whatever the cost to ourselves—may be the greatest priestly service of them all right now. So we must keep turning, turning, turning in the direction of discipleship, as women always have. But differently. For as Basho says, we do not seek to follow in the footsteps of those of old. We seek the things they sought. We don't seek to do what they really need. We need much more than that. We need now to do what they really, really need.

Vision

Both Roots and Wings:
Moving the Vatican II Church
Into a New Millennium

Framing these reflections on roots and wings is a story from the Book of Kings. The scripture teaches that "...in those days God called Samuel...." But Samuel did not as yet recognize the voice of God. "Visions," scripture says, "were scarce in those days," and so Samuel went instead to the priest of the temple, saying, "Eli, you called me. Here I am." But Eli said, "I did not call you. Go back to sleep." Finally after Samuel was called three times, Eli, of whom scripture says, "Eli's eyes were growing dim," instructed Samuel to say, "Lord, here I am." And Samuel did, and what the Lord told Samuel was that Eli's days as high priest were over because there were elements in the old system that had to be changed, things his sons did which Eli had not corrected. What can we possibly think about such a serious situation as this? What can we possibly learn from it in our own time?

First, we must remember that Eli was going blind. Eli was no longer able to see what needed to be done next. But one thing you can say for Eli: Eli, the institution itself, enabled Samuel, taught Samuel, ordered Samuel to hear beyond the institution to the voice of God in his life. And more than that. We must realize that the voice of God to Samuel was that the very institution that had formed him was to be re-formed by him. What Eli had taught him he was to use to correct Eli's world. No doubt about it: Samuel is the saint of Vatican II.

The Jewess, Bella Lewitzky, woman of a wandering people, once wrote, "To move freely you must be deeply rooted." Without doubt, roots and wings are of a piece. One without the other is bogus. To renew the church we must be faithful to the church, and to renew the church we must stretch the church. The question is simply, Stretch it to what? And how?

In what way is the call of Vatican II still current? Is religion itself really of urgent value in today's world? Is organized religion worth the struggle? At its best, religion offers more than a list of answers. Like Eli, it tenders a way to deal with the questions that plague our lives. This transition from certainty to faith, from faithful answers to faithful questions is a slow one. It is the transition from roots to wings. It is the difference between Call to Action 1976 and Call to Action 2001.

Call to Action 1976 was an attempt to make real what was clearly present in the then fresh documents of Vatican II. Call to Action 2001 is a call to make present what is not so clearly evident in the now old documents of Vatican II but is still implied in them, and must still be alive in us if we are to remain as committed to development as we are faithful to our roots. As committed to our roots as we are faithful to development.

Thanks to Vatican II, ideas changed and that frightened some people. It cast others adrift, plunged many into blind resistance. But it energized the rise of another whole church for whom the past was the glue needed to reconfigure a healthier future. Essence remained: 1. God is. 2. Openness to the world is the way of Jesus, and 3. the Holy Spirit lives in each of us. Those are the givens, the things that do not change. Those are the roots that give us wings. In fact, on those ideas has rested the unity of the church and the development of the faith for centuries as the world tilted and turned.

And the world around us, like the world after Galileo and the world after the Enlightenment and the world after the fall of the monarchies in Europe, is shifting like a glacier in sunlight. Now, in our time, we have again a culture in flux and questions in embryo, and gods in conflict, and tensions—personal, social, local, global, international, organizational—aplenty. The question is not whether the faith is believable. The real question is whether that faith is meaningful to us, here and now. We live in a desert between two places: one at the brink of Vatican II, just over the edge of Vatican I, a relatively static world where change and doubt were little tolerated. The other, this world, a borderless world exploding with information, bristling with independence, inundated with questions, teeming with the agitation and the rage of the oppressed and invisible.

The world races blindly by us unsure what, if anything, religion has to offer a wounded, worried, weary world that is awash in clonings and stem cell research, comic book star-wars weapons and the desperate poverty that militarism and nuclear holocaust breed—and now fear, great fear, and houses divided against themselves with a microcosm of world religions in every major city in the world. The world is now a place that prays in many languages at one time.

What are we to be about in church renewal if the church itself is to keep pace? The 25th anniversary questions for Call to Action must be: Why must the church be in the world? How must the church be in the world? And what must the church do now to really be a leavening presence in such a world?

The situation is fraught with danger. It seems we are being asked to ignore the obvious and abandon the vision of Vatican II. On the other hand, we find ourselves without the moorings of the soul it takes to stay a course in dark times, to trust that the Holy Spirit is working in this confusion. But such a situation is not a new one.

In ancient times, when Greek mythology ceased to satisfy the new commitment to the orderly, rational pursuit of evidence, philosophers then, too, began to point out the contradictions inherent in popular theology. Who was really God if there were many gods?

What kind of religion was it that dealt with humanity in some kind of brutal sport? What was heaven if competition between the gods was par for the course, and chaos part and parcel of godliness there? The old myths condemned themselves by their own hand. Intelligent people began to feel distant from a system that was arbitrary and incongruent, destructive and unyielding. Religion reeled from the assault. Philosophy emerged with more reasonable answers to the problems of life than did religion.

Religion as the ancient Greeks had known it was dead. But which was the greater errancy, the mythological explanations of life given by religion or the rational imaginings of the new purveyors of philosophical ideas? In fact, which is the greater errancy today, the distance from the world of a clerical church under siege before Vatican II, or the wildly committed imaginings of the "people of God" after it?

The answer lies now, I think, as it did then, in the relationship between roots and wings, between respect for the past and commitment to the present. Social turbulence is always a sure sign that the faith must be rethought, reinterpreted, restated in the light of present circumstances. It is not the first time in Catholic history that new spiritual understandings have emerged in the light of new questions, and new questions in the light of new understandings. The Council of Nicaea in 325, the Council of Constantinople in 381, the Athanasian Creed in the sixth century, even Pope Paul VI's "Credo of the People of God," published as late as 1968, all attempted, in the face of different questions, to reformulate the fundamentals in ways that could be understood by people at that time.

To question is not to deny. It may, in fact, be the truest type of faith, the most faithful kind of religion. If we are really to be faithful, to be rooted, we must ask ourselves again and again: What did Vatican II really mandate? Those are our roots. And what is left to be done? Those are the things that must give us wings.

Against what must we struggle? And from what can we draw hope? The answer lies in looking again at the *Documents of Vatican II*, with both their turning points and tensions.

1. In the *Dogmatic Constitution on the Church*, the turning point is the very definition of the church itself. In Baltimore Catechism days, the definition was structural and very straightforward. "The church," every child learned, "was that body of lawfully baptized faithful who accepted the teachings of the church, were gathered around the local bishop who was in communion with the church in Rome."

Vatican II enlarged that definition of church, gave us new roots. The church, the council declared, is "the people of God." There and then the focus shifts beyond the hierarchical, beyond spiritual childhood, beyond being consumers of faith to being carriers of faith. But then the tensions multiply too. The whole question of role definitions—of who does what, of gifts and responsibilities, of who's in charge of what, of relationships and ecclesiology, of who is more important than whom in the church—become new points of theological departure.

People who do not "belong" to a church but who "are" the church begin to take that focus seriously and in ways that alter past patterns and beliefs. They begin to make clear that they want their church open to women, open to homosexuals, open to married priests, open to women priests and preachers, open to lay consultation. In other words, they want their wings.

2. In the *Dogmatic Constitution on Divine Revelation* the place of scripture in Catholic formation re-energized literary exegesis and historical scholarship, areas dormant in Roman circles for eons. This fresh encouragement of biblical study raises new issues as well. Whether or not revelation is ongoing may become even more problematic now. Consequently, an understanding of "tradition" that is based on historical patterns of practice and custom is now being contested in favor of new insights with firm scriptural foundation. If scripture, for instance, has nothing at all to say about the ordination of women, on what basis do we use Jesus as our right to obstruct it? It is the question of the place of scripture, the model of Jesus, in the development of doctrine that must give us all new wings.

3. The turning point in the *Constitution on the Sacred Liturgy,*

with its institution of the vernacular as an "official" language of consecration, was its concern to return the liturgy of the church to the people, who are the church. Gone was the notion that Eucharist was something done for us and on us instead of with us, something for a single priest in a dark crypt to "get in." It was all a great breakthrough for Christian community. But tensions lurk in these shadows, too. Uniformity, that long-heralded counterpoint of Catholic unity, became a point of contention about the nature of tradition.

When the bishops called the first Call to Action conference 25 years ago, I sat on the smallest committee, the committee on language. I told the committee that ours was the most volatile topic.

"Impossible," they told me. But the office of women's concerns, altar girls, theological study—these passed. Ours didn't. Our request for two tiny words to designate the whole human race didn't pass. The liturgy became a battleground where bread recipes, the gender, dress and geography of altar servers and ministers became theologically central and the translations of pronouns were centers of conflict and control. Mystique has again become confused with mystery. If we do not get beyond this, there will be no Eucharistic wings on which to fly.

4. In the *Pastoral Constitution on the Church in the Modern World*, the church in Vatican II turned squarely from an insular perspective which emphasized the separateness of the sacred and the secular, to the consideration of the integrity, the essential connectedness of the sacred and the secular. It was a transfiguring moment, never more than now. From a posture of resistance and rejection of the larger world, the church turned to a commitment to human advancement, to the development of world community, to the acceptance of science and to a new concern for the economic and cultural development of all peoples as well as for their spiritual salvation. The transformation of society, in other words, is publicly declared in this key document as an essential part of the church's mission to humanity.

And so the tensions are clear. Someone must still ask, How

much involvement is too much involvement of church in the political system and political issues? When does advocacy become control? And when we argue for moral principles in the market-place, whose morality shall it be and who decides? And how? By endorsing candidates, by forbidding the support of a candidate to people, to adults, to citizens of conscience—or by teaching principles? The answers are slow in coming but on them lies the very existence of wings.

5. The *Decree on Ecumenism* recognized officially the scandal of Christian division. What is more, this statement asserts a unity in vision and essential commitment among the whole Christian family. Finally, the paper affirms the diversity of gifts—liturgical, spiritual and theological—that make up the whole church of Christ in all its denominations. But the challenge is to move Christian ecumenism beyond ecclesiastical get-togethers to the recognition of the single mission and the common table of the total Christian church. The scandal of division is not the scandal of the people. It is the scandal of professional church makers and it must be repented before we can teach peace to anyone else. Indifferentism is not ecumenism, of course, but absolutism, on the other hand, erodes the witness of the full Christian presence, even when it comes packaged in documents from Rome. Conversion and repentance are imperatives of the church as well as its members.

Whatever recent documents, written again without the approbation of the church universal, say to the contrary about the salvific value of our sister churches, Vatican II and its outreach to the entire Christian dispensation is the root that gives the faith wings.

6. In the *Decree on the Bishops' Pastoral Office in the Church,* the church makes a screeching turn from medieval hierarchy to modern pastor. The bishop is not defined in these documents as "lord and lawgiver." His role is to enable the church, to be in touch with issues and ideas, to create a national identity. Clearly the question of international control of the newly heightened local church is the high water to be negotiated now. Without resolving this, pastoral paralysis will surely set in, ecclesiastical climbing for official

favor will surely take over as bishops defer to Roman control rather than stand for national needs, until, in the end, bishops become unnecessary at all. To fly in the face, for instance, of national conferences of bishops and their authorization of liturgical translations for their own countries, let alone attempt to stop the renovation of a cathedral in midair, is not only to obviate the local church but to turn bishops into altar boys as well. It is to tie the wings we have been given.

7. The Vatican II *Decree on the Ministry and Life of Priests* and the *Decree on Priestly Formation* may someday be seen as pivotal to the development of the new church to which the earlier documents point. In these documents clericalism dies an official death, however prevalent it may still be. What is asked of the priest is, of course, the ability to form community, to lead the search for God but to acknowledge, to listen to and to trust the laity whose gifts, the same documents say, are essential to the church. As the telling phrase of the documents, "Brother among brothers" (sic), celebrates, the priest is to be spiritual catalyst, not parish potentate. But the role revision sounds a great deal easier in theory than it is in practice. "Father says" is no longer enough to qualify for the running of a school, a ministry, or a parish unilaterally. From a position of "father," the patriarchal lawgiver of a Roman family in whose hands lie the life or death of the entire clan, the priest is now asked to assume the role of "brother," the documents say, of caring peer, of loving equal—even to the married and to women.

8. The *Decree on the Appropriate Renewal of Religious Life* came over 400 years after the Council of Trent thought it had cast religious life in stone by declaring solemnly that it was just right as it was, wimples, walls and all. No more ministries to consider, no more forms to create, no new orders to allow, no new rules to permit beyond those of the early orders—and then the Council called Vatican II called religious life to renew itself. More importantly, perhaps, the Council instructed religious to turn to the gospels, the initiating intent of their founders and the social realities of the times, not to church law or episcopal control, for their

criteria and direction. And these are dangerous directions all. The tensions surfaced almost immediately and are with us still. The dualistic notion that the essence of religious perfection lies in separation from the world and blind, military obedience, lingers pathologically in the minds of a generation formed on false or symbolic asceticisms rather than on the searing demands of a gospel that cures lepers, raises women from the dead and contends with Scribes and Pharisees from the temple to the tomb.

Transcending the world, then, becomes a counterweight to transforming it. So the renewal of religious life becomes a struggle to balance the claims of law against the touchstone of an experience rife with new poor, alive with new questions, challenged by new kinds of spirituality and spiritual adults. As a result, of the ministries listed in the Kennedy Directory, the registry of official Catholic organizations, over 75 percent were founded by religious communities while they were being called into chanceries and scolded for leaving the schools and not wearing religious uniforms.

Finally the question of whether or not religious life is to be fundamentally charismatic or functionally institutional simmers at the center of the renewal of religious life. Whether religious are to animate or simply to staff the works they undertake in a church in whom all are called to minister and lead and teach and serve remains a determining issue. Are women religious to be the good sisters, the darling daughters of the church, or the dangerous women sent from the tomb with a message on their minds and a gospel in their hands? The struggle between control and charism is getting stronger every day as religious use their roots to justify their wings.

9. That the role of the laity in the church was even an issue at Vatican II may be the greatest turning point of the church's modern history. In the *Decree on the Apostolate of the Laity* the lay state in the church began, for the first time in history, to be described as a "vocation." The laity were instructed in this document that the believer "has both a right and a duty to use their gifts" in the church. Participation rather than passivity became a factor of lay commitment. From that rationale came the call to the laity to be

responsible for church organization, for Catholic education, for religious formation programs, for church administration and for thoughtful, considered reflection, for the *sensus fidelium* that John Henry Newman gifted to the modern church.

The inherent tension in this development of the laity is at least twofold. This departure from clericalism raises the issue of authority. When competency lies with the lay leader, to what degree is the priest in charge of parish or school, and why? Secondly, if the laity really are gifted for the sake of the Christian community, does this mean lay women, too, or only lay men? And if it does mean women, why are they not being generally, wholly, totally accepted in worship or administration, in the diaconate, at least, for which we have centuries of women deacons as models? Here history, theology and law all come together to confront and expose the debilitating sexism of the church. If I were a Roman Catholic bishop in this country, I would not be disturbed that Catholic women were throwing themselves on the steps of the cathedrals begging to minister in the church. I would be disturbed that they had to go to Protestant seminaries for the theological and pastoral preparation to do it.

If Roman Catholic dioceses continue to refuse to prepare women for participation in the church, I predict that this movement of Catholic women to Protestant schools of theology will significantly alter the shape of the church, the faith, in the next 25 years. The preparation of the laity guarantees that the church will always have the wings it needs.

10. In the *Decree on the Church's Missionary Activity,* the turning point is attitudinally so deep that perhaps only a Catholic can sense its real depth. Two new postures are affirmed here. The first is that conversion must be free. With this statement hundreds of years of church-state control are abandoned by a church whose entire middle history was embedded in theocratic governments. The second notion is that missionaries are to be more presence than proselytizers. They are to become inculturated, and, as quickly as possible, enable the new church to become a native church. According to the document, at least, Western ecclesiasti-

cal imperialism is finally over.

However, this growing shift in the center of the church from First to Third World peoples in population, character and tone has done little or nothing to dislodge Roman curial control. Tension is inherent here. How long new native churches will tolerate Western formulations, Western interpretations, Western liturgical forms and Western theological analysis is anybody's guess. The Chinese church, in fact the entire Asian church, and that other newly recognized mission church—the American one—are growing wings.

11. The *Declaration on the Relationship of the Church to Non-Christian Religions* is a time bomb waiting to go off. In a dramatic move, this declaration from a council of the church, solemnly assembled, asserts that as Christians we must accept "all that is true and holy" in non-Christian religions. Imagine! We are clearly saying that in Buddhism, in Hinduism, in Judaism, in Islam there is something "true and holy." After centuries of their repudiation, moreover, the church officially condemns in this statement any persecution or discrimination based on race, color, condition of life or religion. The implications for world development and the creation of human community are far-ranging but late and incomplete: late for Tissa Balasuriya and his call to watch the language of original sin in cultures that see original perfection, late for gays and lesbians who are yet to be seen more as normal than "disordered," late for women who are still considered outside the pale of a God who parts the seas, draws water from a rock and raises the dead to life, but cannot and will not work through a woman. Apparently femaleness is the only substance before which God goes impotent.

More, no consciousness of the effects of pluralism in the new multi-cultural governments is found in this document. The issues of school prayer and the hanging of Judeo-Christian commandments in US courtrooms as the basis for judicial norms, in a government based on the separation of church and state, both of which are now emerging with a vengeance, threaten the very pluralism which, as a nation, we espouse and as a global people we can no longer avoid. The tensions residual in both those realities are yet to be recognized as issues of faith but are, I submit, very real indicators of the presence or absence of true Christians. It is no longer learning to function as a Christian in a non-Christian world that is essential. It is learning to function as a Christian in a non-Christian neighborhood that is essential to the integrity of both state and church.

12. In the *Declaration on Religious Freedom* the revolutionary tenet is simply that conscience must be the primary determinant of religious conviction. Everyone, everyone—even nuns and priests, I assume—is immune from coercion in the name of religion.

The problem is clear: Someone, somewhere must come to grips with coercion. Is legislative pressure or church-state collusion to write denominational morality into law "coercion"? And, if it isn't, whose morality shall it be in a multicultural society in a world without borders? What is the line between church and state? What is the place for conscience in individuals and what does that have to do with the development of doctrine and the measure of our own Catholicity? Who does the measuring?

People do not question because they reject the church. They question the church because they love the church. They question because they seek a spiritual life, with or without an institution, and even outside of it, if being in it is what makes the spiritual life impossible for them. Most of all, they question because the church itself has created an ideal which too often it then does not itself seek. That is what happened to Martin Luther, and Catherine of Siena, and Dorothy Day, and Thomas Merton. They did not question because they did not believe what the church taught, they questioned because they did.

And that's what happened to you and me. They taught the unity-making dimensions of the Eucharist and we believed it. They taught the holy-making power of scripture and we believed it. They taught the community-making power of the church and we believed it. They taught equality and we believed it. In Vatican II they taught a whole new way of being church—and we believed them.

Being rooted in Vatican II is not enough to make yourself a Vatican II Catholic. It is just as necessary to develop Vatican II as it is to preserve it, to grow its wings as to prune its branches. And each of these documents of Vatican II cries out yet for wings by believers who are as committed to the present and dedicated to the future as they are rooted in the past.

For the next 25 years it is not necessary to repeat the agenda of Vatican II, but to complete it. We are struggling now with silencings for thinkers and *mandatums* for theologians, and recipes for liturgy and a newly emerging authoritarian pastoring and a parallel priesthood independent of local bishops and more committed to some transcendent ideology than to the enculturation of the local church—a system to be reckoned with in the future, mark my word.

But there are signs of great hope, as well. There are lay theologians now who speak a bold truth. There are groups who know they are the new church in embryo: Dignity and the Association for the Rights of Catholics in the Church and Women's Ordination Conference. Quixote Center and Pax Christi and the Center of Concern and the Leadership Conference of Women Religious and Conference of Major Superiors of Men. And especially Call to Action, you—this great flowing movement of faithful hearts. There is, most of all, the Holy Spirit who refuses to give up on us. And finally there is Samuel, who allowed the institution to lead him to the voice of God and then built a new people in the shadows of the old. There are the wings that come from Vatican II itself to carry us—because of our roots—beyond our roots. The message of Vatican II at this 25th anniversary moment is still: Go on! Fly, church, fly!

Prophecy

*Thomas Merton: Seeder of Radical
Action and the Enlightened Heart*

To talk about a well-published monk from a cloistered community who has been dead more than thirty years presumes two questions: First, how was he different? And secondly, so what?

Thomas Merton's patchwork life is a comfort to the average person. It is at the same time a confusion. Merton was a precocious child, an out-of-control youth, a dissipated young man, a college playboy, an intellectual. Thomas Merton was not the boy next door. He was a man who walked the path from hell to heaven, exposing the journey at every turn so that the rest of us could find hope and meaning in our own journey.

There are several stories that may best explain the influence and the place of Thomas Merton in contemporary society and spiritual development. Two are from the Sufi masters; one is from a personal source.

Once upon a time, the first story tells, some disciples begged their old and ailing master not to die.

"But if I do not go, how will you ever see?" the Master said to them. "But what is it we can possibly see when you are gone?" With a twinkle in his eye, they say, the Master answered, "All I ever did in my entire life was to sit on the river bank handing out river water. After I'm gone, I trust that you will notice the river."

The lesson rings true. What teachers teach us while they live is one thing; the quality of what they leave us to think about for the rest of our lives is another. Thomas Merton was a fascinating, engaging, offbeat, charming and provocative personality, true. But what he directed the world to see was far more than the mystique, the mystery of the cloistered life. He left us things worth thinking about for a long, long time.

In the second story, a seeker said to the Master, "Master, I am intent on the spiritual life. May I become your disciple?" And the Master answered, "You are only a disciple because your eyes are closed. The day you open them you will see that there is nothing you can learn from me or anyone else." "But if that is the case," the seeker said, "what then is a master for?" "The purpose of a master," the Holy One replied, "is to make you see the uselessness of having one."

Thomas Merton's legacy was surely to make us see beyond himself, to bring us to see the rivers around us, to enable us to understand the difference between piety and spirituality, between pseudo and real contemplation, as he did.

The third story is about a fifteen-year-old who read only one "holy" book in the entire sophomore year of high school, and that by accident. The book was called *Seeds of Contemplation* and the youngster discovered at a much later date that that one book had made everything in life look different.

In fact, Merton leaves all of us with two masterful challenges—to discover the world around us and to find the contemplative spirit within. He did it from a difficult distance, and he did it, at that time, almost alone in a world whose piety was private and whose religion was ritual. He did it in the face of a World War II generation whose sense of life had been jaded by a pervasive presence of violent death, whose idea of development had become unrestrained consumption, whose religion had been sin, sorrow, repentance and petition for favors from a vending machine and American god, whose notion of freedom was untrammeled individualism, uncritical Americanism and uncontested international messianism. Merton, the monk, was a leading critic of nuclearism, a voice for nonviolence in a time of civil strife, a pathfinder in east-west inter-religious dialogue, a model of globalism, a member of the International Fellowship of Reconciliation, a theologian of ecology, a social analyst, a public figure, a man with an awareness of the feminine dimension of God. On the last day of his life in Bangkok at a conference of Benedictine and Cistercian abbots he told us, "The monastic is essentially someone who takes up a critical attitude toward the world and its structures...saying that the claims of the world are fraudulent."

He was, in other words, a genuine contemplative who left insights enough to seed an entire generation in both contemplation and action. Thomas Merton was clearly another kind of monk. Merton was a monastic whose monasticism sprang from a single-minded search for God in life rather than from a single-minded escape from the world for life in God, as ironic as that may seem coming from a cloistered monk.

Merton's monasticism was a revolution equaled only by the origin of Benedictine monasticism itself. Until the 6th century, monasticism had been an exercise in private and personal spirituality. It was Benedict who, in the 6th century, made human community itself the essence of sanctity. Merton's monasticism, too, was a revolution that took monasticism out of the confines of the local monastery and situated it in a concern for world community itself. Merton's monasticism was a monasticism concentrated on the presence of God in the present.

Merton saw the world through a heart uncluttered by formulas and undimmed by systems. He taught more than piety and asceticism for its own sake. He taught concepts that flew in the face of tradition then and fly in the face of culture still: the sin of poverty, the moral imperative of peace, the rectitude of stewardship, the holy power of nonviolence, the sanctity of globalism, and the essence of enlightenment. Merton sowed seeds of contemplation that led to action—an often forgotten but always bedrock spiritual concept.

In Jewish spirituality, for instance, two concepts dominate and are intertwined: The one, *devekut*, translates as "clinging to God" or contemplation; the other, *tikkun o'lam*, translates "repairing the world" or the work of justice. One without the other—contemplation without justice, clinging to mystery without repairing the real world—is unfinished, the tradition teaches, is dark without light, is grand without great, is soul without body.

Scripture is equally clear about the concept as well. Samuel, Solomon, Abraham and David, Judith and Esther, Mary and Mary Magdalene, Matthew, Mark, Luke, John, Peter and Paul all cling to God, all converse with God. All contemplate the presence of God in life and all of them are called to do something about it.

Contemplation, Merton teaches us, is learning to see the world as God sees the world. The contemplative sees the world through the eyes of God and the real contemplative is driven to respond according to the mind of God for it. Clinging to God, in other words, generates the passion it takes to repair the world. Merton's monastic contemplation joins those two concepts again, this time in the face of a culture that is inclined more to rituals than to this kind of contemplative dimension of religion.

Indeed, Merton spent his life dealing out river water to a world yet disinclined to see the river itself but claiming to be following it. Merton handed out river water to soften the dry and sterile ground of religion gone hard, and life gone barren. In *Seeds of Contemplation*, his earliest work, Merton shows us six rivers still running today, still needing our attention: poverty, militarism, ecological stewardship, nonviolence, globalism and the enlightenment that is contemplation.

Poverty and the depths of human indignity it spawns is a river Merton wants us to see. It is in *Seeds of Contemplation* that Merton writes, "Even the desire of contemplation can be impure when we forget that true contemplation means the complete destruction of all selfishness...." It is in *Seeds of Contemplation*, then, that we first come to realize that behind Merton we must come to see the river of poverty that flows outside the pale of a pseudo-contemplation and cloaks itself selfishly in the mysterious and the unreal as a way to avoid God where God really is: in the people who need us.

Consequently, we have a culture seemingly religious that talks soaringly about the lives of its successful but has little or no ear at all for the sagas of those whose lives weave a lesser tale, a culture that sees even religion as the comfort of the self. As a result, some of us find the world a wonderful place to live in. Our newspapers record our progress, our statues remember our public heroes, our cities enshrine our economic temples. But Fifth Avenue is light years away from Harlem. Trump Towers, where the rich live, is a planet removed from the train tunnels under it where the homeless live. The White House is an entire culture away from the people who have no money, no clout, no power, no highly paid lobbyists to make their case.

The wealthy, Alan Durning writes in *The State of the World*, in the '90s have seen the value of their goods increase 20 times since 1900, the products of their industries 50 times and their personal travel 1,000 times. Yet, the disparities between the rich and poor of the world have widened obscenely. In the 1990s, this world housed 157 billionaires, and over two million millionaires, but it did not house 100 million homeless at all, while we go to church and we go to church and we go to church. What kind of contemplation is that? What kind of religious action is that?

In this country alone, we spend five billion dollars each year to lower our calorie consumption while 400 million people around the world cannot eat at all and so waste away with starved bodies or live with underfed and stunted brains—people we then call "dumb," "stupid," "incapable," "illiterate," "uneducated," "uncouth"— while we hoard grain in barns to use as political power against those for whom death is a happier thought than life. The river of poverty runs through New Delhi and Manila and through New York and Chicago and Miami, as well. Where are the contemplatives who will leave their churches and open their hearts long enough to cling to God by repairing the effects of poverty? Because if we do not, Merton warns us, "Even the desire for contemplation will be impure."

Militarism is a river Merton wants us to see. Behind Merton, we must also come to see the river of pain that is caused by the warmongers of the world and which flows alongside the chanting churchgoers who see God outside the world instead of within it. Merton insisted in *Seeds of Contemplation*, "People who know nothing of God and whose lives are centered on themselves imagine that they can only 'find themselves' by asserting their own desires and ambitions and appetites in a struggle with the rest of the world...." And our age, perhaps, has done it best, and done it globally while we protest that we are a nation under God.

Both the bishop of Boston and the bishop of Baghdad, for instance, called the war in the Persian Gulf "just." Surely there is something wrong either with the theory or with the theology of those who call themselves religious if the theory of the just war can be read totally differently and with the same ease by all sides at the same time.

In our time, too, for the first time in history, we have justified the extermination of women and children on the grounds that indiscriminate assaults against civilians saves soldiers. It is time, surely, to contemplate the possibility that what we really need to contemplate now, in our time, is a theory of the "unjust war."

And what we have not destroyed with weaponry itself—an army of over 200,000 Iraqis in the Persian Gulf alone, for instance—we have destroyed simply by the making of those weapons. We have used our best minds, our best resources, and the bulk of our national budget to build what will destroy people rather than to build what will develop them. "Our policy," Secretary Cohen said in August of 1998, "is significant force." Indeed we have seduced our industries, our university system and even the religious community into equating security with militarism. And we have paid a great price for it. To satisfy our vampire's appetite for militarism, we have threatened the level of human services available in this country: schools, hospitals, housing, welfare, the arts. We have absorbed the resources of other nations that it takes to make or base our weapons and so dimmed the hopes of the children of the future.

According to over thirty research organizations in the United States, during that six-week war we fought so gloriously in the Gulf in 1991, here at home 1,240 children died from the effects of poverty; 4,000 infants died due to low birth weight; 68,750 young people dropped out of school; and 4,000 workers became unemployed—all conditions we say we now can't afford to fix. Clearly, war kills everyone, even those who are lucky enough to win it. As long as mothers in Iraq, punished by sanctions aimed at men, go on to this day giving their choleric children water from rivers running with garbage and thick with human excrement we are, at best, only pseudo-contemplative.

In Vietnam, they inflated the number of casualties and conquests to affect victory. In the Gulf War they at least showed us corpses in burned-out jeeps in the searing desert. In Afghanistan they are showing us nothing at all—except the hole in the middle of our own New York. There are no refugee camps, no estimate of the number of Afghan civilians whose lives have also been ended, one way or another, by the collapse of their country and its non-stop pummeling. Oh, every once in a while a picture seeps through the net: an Afghan baby eating a mudpie made of grass "and a trace of wheat flower" because of the food shortage, a child whose leg has been amputated by a land mine, a village in rubble.

After days, months, of non-stop bombing we are apparently, somehow, waging a war without victims. At great cost. With no public discussion of its internal implications for either country—and countries around the globe—other than the fact that we were hit and so we hit "them" back. Worse, anyone who tries to discuss other dimensions of the situation is called "unpatriotic." Writers lose their jobs. Peace groups who plead for less barbaric means of conflict resolution in a world dangerous to itself are ridiculed. A terrible silence reigns. A fearful silence reigns.

The fact may be that we lose as much as we win in war. We lose our humanity, perhaps, because we have failed to contemplate that the river of pain that runs through the world cannot be staunched by force and the failure of reason.

Ecological stewardship is a river Merton wants us to see.

Behind Merton, because of Merton, we must come to see the river of human debris that gushes past the pious "contemplatives" who substitute praying for a prayerful respect for the cycle of nature and the circle of life. "A tree gives glory to God first of all by being a tree," Merton taught us in *Seeds of Contemplation*. "This particular tree will give glory to God," Merton went on, "by spreading out its roots in the earth and raising its branches into the air and the light in a way that no other tree before or after it ever did or ever will do." "The special clumsy beauty of this particular colt...this particular April sky...that great, gashed, half-naked mountain are all holy in the sight of God, all imitate God," Merton wrote.

But one at a time, we are destroying them, unconsciously, carelessly, callously. We are missing the river. But we call ourselves religious, disciples, a chosen people "under God." "Life is the greatest bargain," the Yiddish proverb says, "we get it for nothing." But we have come to treat it as nothing, too. We have spoiled our nests as no animal would do and we justify it in the name of "maintaining a standard of living" that is making the globe unlivable and being human inhumane.

Air pollution was cited by scientists as a serious problem in the early '70s. The data was clear then. A political commitment to curb industrial waste that would soften campaign coffers or lose votes or yield international economic supremacy however, definitely was not.

According to scientist Hilary French in a 1990 World Watch report, severe health problems related to air pollution now cover the globe. In the United States, French says, 150 million people, over half the population of the country, breathe air considered unhealthy by the environmental protection agency. In Hungary, every seventeenth death is caused by air pollution. In India, French confirms, breathing the air in Bombay is equivalent to smoking ten cigarettes a day. And in Mexico, the capital city with notoriously noxious air is considered, irony of ironies, a hardship post for diplomats of countries who go to conferences on the environment but refuse to agree to pollution standards that would clear it up. The environmental impacts are even more startling: acid rain and air pollution are decimating crops and devastating forests and destroying lakes and buildings, too, even in the industrialized countries of the world. "Till the garden and keep it," the scripture mandate, has become "seize the garden and rape it." And we have yet to elevate the survival of the globe to the level of a moral concern.

Nonviolence is a river Merton wants us to see. Behind Merton, because of Merton's call to contemplation, we must come to see as well the river of nonviolence. Real contemplatives know all creation to be a piece of God's presence in the world and so to be reverenced and treated tenderly. Violence has simply run its course: War is now obsolete. War is much more than conflict, it is social annihilation. Human relations on such grand scale require cooperation, not coercion.

What we destroy we defeat, true, but most of all we destroy something in ourselves. What we do to one another gouges out the center of our own lives. To napalm children is to pour acid on my own soul. To pulverize a nation in just 43 days as we did in Iraq, to turn cities to ash in minutes, is not to make life cheap, it is to make life vulgar.

To bomb an innocent people, an illiterate people, a destitute people into tent cities on foreign borders as we did in Afghanistan, babies in their bellies and old people on their backs, is obscene. We will starve out a half million people tonight, another three million soon, seven million, the entire population of New York City, by the end of the winter, if the call of Oxfam, Cafod, Christian Aid, Islamic Relief and the Muslim Public Affairs Council for a humanitarian pause in the bombing during Ramadan is ignored. To reject the cry to deliver food to people living on vegetation while we eat carrot cake, while we boast that we are not targeting civilians, is to shift the moral question away from terrorism to the integrity of bombing.

To duplicate in them what has happened to us, in order to show their governments—the very people we put in place, the very people whose control we engineered—that we will not tolerate their resistance to our plans and policies, is not to bring justice to the world. It is simply to continue the cycle of vengeance on the innocent which will live on against us in their children while the violent still go free. Or as the Roman philosopher Seneca said of it: "They make a desert and call it peace."

War has become the pitting of one group of invisible combatants against another group of defenseless noncombatants and cannot therefore possibly be called "just" by any theological measure, here or anywhere else.

To refuse restraint, to subordinate focused search and capture missions, stronger financial strategies, heightened international intelligence work, increased domestic security to carpet bombing, cluster bombs and cruise missiles, raises serious moral questions about the effect of localized force on tiny cells of international terrorists somewhere else.

To refuse nonviolent means of conflict resolution, to set up commissions and committees of war chiefs and warlords, military advisors and consultants, and have not so much as one member of the peace academy, not one expert in nonviolent conflict resolution at the table, not one refugee, not one woman who will be the real victims of such "justice" be part of the assessment of a policy is to determine the outcome without asking the question.

To refuse to sign protocols that would set up a world court and then wonder why there is no world coalition when justice is needed most, to take away civil rights of privacy, law, and citizenship in the name of protecting civil rights, to practice fascism in the name of democracy is to mock what we say we stand for. It is to destroy by our own hands what we say we are securing.

And then to wonder why guns become the playthings of children, or why families are torn apart by domestic murders, or why women are routinely beaten, or why drugs become the desensitizer of choice in a world where violence is social and economic and domestic policy as well as military, is to raise denial to the level of high art. Indeed, the blood of our own children runs red in our streets because we have taught our children violence very well—and they have learned it quickly. We are reaping what we have sown. We are getting what we asked for.

How can we possibly convince them that their violence is bad but our violence is good if we keep justifying the decimation of peoples in the name of God?

Into that climate of nationalism and chauvinism and unholy righteousness came Thomas Merton in *Seeds of Contemplation* with waters of loving nonviolence. "To say that I am made in the image of God," Merton says, "is to say that love is the reason for my existence, for God is love." "Because God's love is in me," he wrote to us, "it can come to you from a different and special direction that would be closed if God did not live in me...and because it is in both of us, God has greater glory. God's love is expressed in two more ways in which it might not otherwise be expressed."

"Violence in a house," the rabbis say, "is like a worm in fruit." It destroys what otherwise looks healthy and firm and good but which is harboring within it the cause of its own decline. Violence is eating the heart right out of this country—in private homes and police stations, in personal relationships, playgrounds and public policies. Violence is our national disease. Walking gently through life is our only real hope of gentling the world. God's love, Merton teaches us, can only come through me. The love of God for which I seek can only come through you.

Globalism is a river Merton wants us to see. Behind Merton, we must come to see as well the river of globalism that flows through the real contemplatives who find God everywhere.

"The more I become identified with God," wrote Merton in *Seeds of Contemplation*, "the more I will be identified with all the others who are identified with God." "We are members one of another," he wrote in an intellectually insular USA, "and everything that is given to one member is given to the whole body."

"The saints are glad to be saints," he told us in a new and powerful insight into sanctity, "not because their sanctity makes them admirable to others but because the gift of sainthood makes it possible for them to admire everybody else..., it delivers them from the burden of judging others and condemning them." And he told us that in a world that suspected almost everybody and saw the world as a place to be evangelized into western culture, US politics, white power and uncurbed capitalism.

He saw the world as good, its many peoples as gifts of the

same God, its religions as many manifestations of the one God, its differences a revelation to the world. He asked us to open our eyes and see what no law ever taught: that life is not a set of boundaries; life is a river of possibilities to be cultivated, a tide of differences to be respected, to be held in awe.

When people are doing our work for wages we ourselves would not accept, we must begin to ask what there is about us that enables us to exploit them. When US industries engage in business practices on the international level that would not be allowed in our own country we must begin to ask, if we are really contemplatives, what is it in our own souls that allows us to treat other people as if they were not people at all. When the resources of the world are controlled by the few, when the mineral deposits of one nation are held hostage by another, we must begin to ask, if we are really contemplatives, whether there isn't already an international welfare system where the poor nations support the rich ones, and haven't we created it while we deny our own poor the same.

Where are the contemplatives like Merton who will begin to see, who will begin to ask at what moral peril we have bought our wealth and our power and our standard of living? "It is God's love that speaks to me in the birds and streams," Merton said in *Seeds of Contemplation*, "...but if God's will would grow from my freedom, I would become the love that God is...." When the starving sick lie dying on subway grates, if I am a contemplative, Merton would say, I must become the love that God is.

When the underemployed workers in Detroit lose their homes and their dignity, I must become the love that God is. When the blacks die in Soweto because they are black, and kill one another in the housing projects of Chicago because they are in despair at being black in a white world, I must become the love that God is. When Iraqi children die in American wars, and crack babies languish on our own streets, if I am really a contemplative, I must become the love that God is.

Globalism, to Merton, is the ability to open my heart and my mind, my arms and my policies to the whole world, not simply the world that is my color, my class. No mastery of past pious disciplines—no matter how time-honored, no matter how good—substitutes, in Merton's mind, for real contemplation, for the ability to see with the eyes of God.

Enlightenment, real contemplation, is a river Merton wants us religious types to see. Merton calls us all to another way of looking at life and another way of living it. Merton calls us, leads us, to the river of enlightenment. "Go into the desert," Merton teaches us in *Seeds of Contemplation,* "not to escape others but in order to find them in God." No amount of religious ritual, no quantity of religious reading, no degrees in religious history will forgive us the responsibility to be religious people, to bind the world together again in God.

Once upon a time, the Sufi tell, a master whose disciples were about to go on the salvific pilgrimage gave them each a bitter gourd to take with them into every holy shrine for every holy prayer. When the disciples returned from their holy and sanctifying journey, the master requested that each of the acrid gourds be cooked for the welcome home dinner. "Ah," the master said, as the disciples gagged on the biting taste, "I see that no amount of holy water has been able to sweeten what was sour."

Over and over again Merton tells us in *Seeds of Contemplation* that simply living the law and repeating the ritual is not enough. Merton calls us to sweeten what is tinged with sharp in us, to repair what is broken in us, to cling to the God who is God, yes, but for the sake of a whole hurting world gone sour, not simply for my own spiritual satisfaction.

The person with the enlightened heart knows that the purpose of the human voice is to give sound to the voiceless until, finally, the world begins to hear what the enlightened heart has come to know—God's presence here, now, in everyone. Where the person stands who has an enlightened heart is more like the reign of God than it was before they got there: the property is beautiful, the litter is gone, the street is safe, the stranger is welcomed, the poor are fed, the refugee is housed, the works of war become works of peace. Nothing else is acceptable to Merton. Nothing else is called holy because any other defilement of life says that the world belongs to me rather than that I and it belong to God.

The person with an enlightened heart is on earth to care for it, not to consume it. The person with an enlightened heart is detached from what holds the world in the grip of money lust and patriarchal power. Once upon a time, the Sufi say, a Holy One said to the businessman, "As the fish perished on dry land, so you perish when you get entangled in the world. The fish must return to the water; you must return to God." The businessman was aghast. "Are you saying that I must give up my business and go into a monastery?" And the Holy One said, "No, no, hold on to your business and go into your heart." Merton's concept of contemplation leads to the same insight: There are two things that corrode the human endeavor: wanting more of everything and never knowing the meaning of enough.

The person with an enlightened heart is emptied of the need to take up all the space and use up all the goods and grind up all the people. No ethnic jokes are ever told by the person with an enlightened heart; no sexist language is ever used; no racial slurs are ever uttered. No enemy bashing is ever practiced. People are people, not colors or sexes or ages or types.

Enlightenment is the ability to see beyond all the things we make God, and find God. We make religion God and so fail to see godliness where religion is other, though goodness is clear and constant in the most different of people, in the remotest of places.

We make national honor God while refugees pour by the thousands through all the porous borders of the world and of every hundred people alive only 30 are white. Which, incidentally, makes whiteness as a norm of anything quite suspect.

We fail to see the presence of God in other nations, particularly non-Christian nations. We make personal security God and fail to see God in others' needs on those bleak and barren days when life seems fragile and our own future unsure.

We make human color and gender the color and gender of God and fail to see God in the one who comes in different shades and other forms, though our scriptures are clear about equality and our theology is sound.

We separate spirit and matter as if they were two different things, though we know now, from quantum physics, that matter is simply fields of force made dense by the spirit of energy that is the base of everything. We are one with the universe, in other words. We are not separate from it or different from it.

And we are not above it. And we are in it—all of us and everything—swimming in an energy that is God. And so we are not separate from one another, or different from each other either. We are, each of us, simply one more sliver of humanity seeking to become more human, trying to be godly, and we will never be it either by diminishing ourselves or by degrading others.

To be enlightened is to see behind all the forms life takes to the God who holds them in being. Enlightenment sees, too, behind the shapes, icons and language that intend to personalize God to the God who is too personal, too encompassing, to be any single shape or form or name.

Enlightenment takes us beyond our parochialisms to the presence of God everywhere, in everyone, in the universe. It ignores color. It disdains gender. It releases gifts and listens to voices not its own precisely because they are not its own.

To be enlightened is to be in touch with the God within us and around us, in ourselves and in others, more than it is to be engulfed in any single way, any one manifestation, any specific denominational or nationalistic or sexual construct, however good, however well-intentioned that kind of benign ungodliness may be.

God is radiant light, blazing fire, asexual spirit, colorless wind. God is the magnet of our souls, the breath of our hearts, the stuff of our lives. God is no one's pigment, no one's flag and no one's gender. And those who certify their God under any of those credentials make a new idol in the desert. To be enlightened we must let God speak to us through everything—and everyone—through whom God shines in life.

It is a practice in many monasteries of my order as we process into chapel for prayer to bow first to the altar, yes, but then to turn and bow to the sister who is walking in procession with us.

The meaning of such a monastic custom, a gesture common to monasticisms around the world, in fact, is clear: God is as much in the world around us, as much in one another, as on that altar or in that chapel. The great ecumenical mind, the great contemplative spirit, the great peacemaking heart magnifies the meaning of that gesture to the level of the universal. It makes visible, demonstrable, present and overpowering the goals for which all religions—Buddhist, Hindu, Jewish, Christian, Muslim—exist.

"The ultimate perfection of the contemplative life," Merton insists, in *Seeds of Contemplation*, "is not a heaven of separate individuals, each one viewing a private vision of God; it is a sea of love.... God is the life of all of us and we are all one in God." We are all one with Nelson Mandela, and we are all one with Yasser Arafat, and we are all one with Saddam Hussein, and we are all one with the children in the squatter's settlements of South Africa, and we are all one with the AIDS patients in the San Francisco hospices, and we are all one with the people in Panama whose homes we destroyed and have yet to restore as we promised. We are all one, the contemplative knows, so it is not just that their salvation depends on us. The fact is that our salvation depends on how we deal with Mandela and McVeigh and Hussein and child murderers whom we have trained to kill. The person with an enlightened heart sees hospitality as the tabernacle of the world. Either God is in the other or God is not, and if God is in the other we dare not leave them out.

There are some things that the contemplative, the person with an enlightened heart, simply will not do because they contribute to the destruction of the world rather than to its development. The person with an enlightened heart, for instance, will not promote weaponry. The person with a monastic heart will not buy a t-shirt or a toy or a bumper sticker or a banner that glorifies war. The person with an enlightened heart will not poison the land or foul the waters or dump waste in foreign countries so that the poor there will die from what makes the wealthy here richer. The person with an enlightened heart advocates for policies that work for the poor and the homeless and the underemployed as well as the secure. The person with an enlightened heart remembers the forgotten generation of children who need day care and lunch and the arts and opportunities of life if the next generation is to have the possibilities and the quality that marked the last. The person with the enlightened heart realizes that the questions of this age cannot be answered with the limited vision of the past.

The person with Merton's enlightened contemplative heart knows that war has gone far beyond the conflict of armies to the ruination of whole civilizations, knows that poverty is not an accident of nature, it is the foreign policy of wealthy nations and the debt crisis of ones made poor due to the ravishing by other ones, knows that the globe is not a cosmic garbage dump, knows that force only triggers force and makes things worse, and that the only thing we have yet to try on violence is nonviolence.

The person with Merton's enlightened contemplative heart knows that the globe has no natural boundaries, only unnatural divisions. Indeed, Thomas Merton has sat on the river bank doling out water for over 50 years. He sowed seeds of contemplation that changed the mentality of the world and sowed the seeds of soul that let loose the force of radical action. Like those Benedictine monastics before him who brought order to a ruined empire and gave agriculture back to a stampeded civilization and reforested the stony valleys of Europe, and saved the learning of the ages by copying the books themselves, Merton hearkens us back to the values that saved civilizations before us so that a civilization desperately in need of peace and nonviolence and stewardship and a sense of the divine in the mundane can be saved again—if we will only see the rivers to which his life points.

It is not an easy task but it has succeeded, if not for all, at least for many; if not for many, at least for me. I do not know who the first master was who was a giver of water. I do not know who the first master was to tell us that there was a religion so religious that it far exceeded the law. But one thing I do know for sure. I know that Merton seeded young hearts as well as old because I was the fifteen-year-old who read *Seeds of Contemplation* fifty years ago and was never the same again.

I learned from Merton, for instance, that the rivers of poverty and war and planetary poison rage around us while we claim religiosity. I also learned that the rivers of peace and nonviolence and globalism are possible if we will only contemplate God long enough, practice *devekut* and *tikkun o'lam* deeply enough, come to see God clearly enough, want God intensely enough to find God where God really is: here, all around us, within us, and within the ones born in stables and driven from the temples of the world, as well. Indeed, contemplation is not an easy task. It cannot be done in isolation. It cannot be done for its own sake.

The Sufi tell the story of the Holy One who was walking along the flooding banks of a raging river when suddenly he saw an arachnid clinging to a tree branch only inches above the swollen stream. "Poor thing," the Holy One said. "Scorpions can't swim. If the waters reach that hanging branch, that spider will surely drown."

And then the Holy One dropped to the ground and began to crawl along the branch toward the spider. But every time the Holy One touched the spider, it stung the hand that reached to rescue it. A passerby said firmly, "Don't you realize that if you try to handle that scorpion, it will sting you?" "Of course," the Holy One said, "but simply because it is the scorpion's nature to sting, does not mean that I should abandon my human nature to save."

Merton shows us a contemplation steeped in action, a clinging to God that demands the repair of the world, an enlightenment that leads to change and hope and holiness. My prayer for people who steep themselves in Merton is that they also steep themselves in a God who is in the world calling us all to a new enlightenment of heart, beyond the law, beyond the books, to a long look at God where God is and where God is not, to the contemplation that leads to action. The ages are full proof: sting it must, this contemplation of God in reality, but for the sake of those who live in hope of a better world, save it will. Sting it must, but save it surely will if we finally come to realize that though nothing we do changes the past, everything we do changes the future.

Peace

*There Just Aren't
Any Just Wars Anymore*

"Better a bad peace than a good war," the saying goes. The question, of course, is What happens if you get neither? Our wars, fought with the most sophisticated war machinery of all time, have yielded neither peace nor noble achievements. The war in Vietnam was intolerable. The defoliation of the country, the devastation of the innocent and the demoralization of the American people counted for nothing. The war in Panama was silly. Thousands were left homeless by an assault aimed at one man who surrendered but could not be captured. The Gulf War was a fiasco: we crushed the crushable at a measure of barbarity unknown in human history. US-led forces expended more explosive tonnage in Kuwait and Iraq in 110 days than was dropped by all sides during all of World War II. "Apocalyptic," the UN report called the bombing, after the fact. "Bombed back into a pre-industrial age," the report said, after the fact.

The problem is that the "victory" was a fiasco, too. Hussein is still in power; Kuwait is still a feudal state; the economic sanctions are still in effect; another people, this time the Kurds, are being displaced and destroyed and war itself has reached a new low.

The TV networks who did not show us that conflict, as they had the war in Vietnam, were finally resuscitated from the comatose state of censorship that was imposed on them during the war—and which they, apparently, gladly accepted, democracy or no democracy—to show us a little, at least, of what a disastrous peace looks like: oil well fires, junkyard deserts, and streams of dirty, dying, desperate and despairing refugees.

The countries that could send sortie after sortie to pulverize the industries and utilities of a civilian population that would suffer from their loss for a generation or more could not, the networks told us, send more than two helicopter flights a day to drop food to its living and innocent victims. The United States built tent cities with inadequate sanitation facilities for thousands of women who were terrified and men who were not soldiers and babies who were dying and families who were displaced by the saturation bombing. Then they went right on selling weapons to the region. The man they characterized as "Hitler" in order to pump the American public up for war, they left in power as another kind of political pawn against, apparently, the possibility of an even worse enemy. They substituted one set of victims for another. They made a mess of peace. They called it "just."

The classical "just war theory" was devised by Augustine to critique the morality of war and to control its process within military parameters. The problem is that the concepts of just cause, competent authorization, comparative justice, right intention and last resort, the characteristics of the "just war," all pale in the face of modern warfare. What cause can possibly be so great as to risk the extermination of life in a region for generations to come? What single nation, however legal its processes, has the right to crush the innocent of another people in the name of political balance and military gain? Who is so totally and perfectly "right" in all circumstances that whatever amount of damage occurs to whatever people in the pursuit of "rightness" is "acceptable collateral damage"? Is the pulverization of an entire area a manifestation of right intentions of peace and reconciliation and reasonable negotiation? Is war ever the only last resort in a world where only some situations are met with maximum force? When the Pol Pot regime in Cambodia decimated its own population, the world did nothing. When the Arab Palestinians were totally dislocated on the West Bank, the world did nothing. When all the blacks of South Africa were reduced to the level of the inhuman, the world did nothing. Why are some places but not others considered bases for war if all the motives are right and all the causes are just?

The world must finally face the question: If this is the text-book definition of a just war, how shall we ever recognize an unjust one? Why is it, if the just war theory really works, that the bishops on each side in a war can with such aplomb pronounce both positions as just? The bishop in Baghdad considered Kuwait the 19th province of Iraq and most of the bishops of the United States found US involvement unworthy of moral condemnation.

Who will give Catholics a theology of the *unjust* war that makes us focus, at the outset, on the *results* of war on innocent people instead of at the precesses of *beginning* one?

Maybe it's time to look into the human heart rather than into tomes of commentaries written for another world at another time, commentaries that treat war as an abstract philosophical problem rather than a human aberration.

We Catholics do not philosophize about abortion, for instance. We simply say it's wrong. We do not philosophize about unjust wages and working conditions. We deplore them. We do not philosophize about infidelity in marriage. We condemn it.

But when it comes to brutal, total, all-out war, we find it impossible to distinguish between AK-47s and nuclear bombs, between self-defense and ecological disaster. We call weapons of planetary destruction a matter of "theological doubt" and refer for justification to the presence of war in the Old Testament, an argument from the past which we would not tolerate in science or medicine or law, for instance. If once-popular approaches to other problems were found to be deficient, we would laugh them to scorn in the interest of enlightenment or progress or discovery. Where war is concerned, on the other hand, we depend for our intellectual and moral approach to a system of thinking that emerged centuries before bombers or missiles or nuclear warheads. We assume that what has been done is what must be done and we simply do it better—or worse actually—than we have ever done it before. What Isaiah decried in the battering ram we now enhance by saturation bombing, but the results are still the same: the innocent are destroyed in great numbers, soldiers become instruments of machines, the powerful calculate their profits in oak-walled rooms while the simple die to enhance their egos and young Americans are turned into the less than civilized who applaud the "turkey shoot" of technological warfare against an over-rated, under-prepared Third World army.

It isn't that war is not nice, as the generals love to say. The fact is that war is inhuman, war is irrational, war is barbaric. War simply cannot be tolerated in civilized society. Surely war cannot be blessed by religion and have the religion itself be real. What Augustine of Hippo gave us in the just war theory was not a justification for war; it was the first organized way of critiquing war. It was implicit moral condemnation of the degradation that war brings under the guise of justice. In this new age it would surely be Augustine most of all who would want us to look again at what is happening to us in the name of military power. The just war theory was a beacon, not a stop light. The last word has not been said on war because the last weapon of war has not been invented.

Up until this time of mass national murders, we have assumed that war could, if it were handled with restraint and integrity, be just. War was, after all, fought under the guise of rules, between armies and under a patina of moral outrage and national righteousness. Now, with the planet in danger and innocent people everywhere being dispossessed or destroyed by the ravages of wars that know no boundaries and recognize no limits, we have to assume that war is basically unjust and simply ask ourselves how much injustice we can stomach in the name of nationalism, national honor and national gain.

As the refugees stream across our television screens and babies die of a diarrhea spawned months before by bombed out water purification systems and an entire nation is starved of the supplies they need to rebuild an economy, an agriculture, an industry while the generals and the soldiers and the politicians who started the war and ran the war and fought the war get ready for Christmas and dressed for Easter, the human conscience cries out for a new set of rules.

I suggest, in the face of modern technology, that we need a new framework in which to evaluate war. We must begin to think more about the effects of war before we start one than we do about the process of having one. Seven areas, in particular, may deserve special attention as we try to define the real moral character of war for us in our new world.

I suggest that the following qualities may be better indicators of the essential injustice of the wars we face than the criteria we have been using to determine that we are not simply being more barbaric in our use of force than the people we face.

I suggest that a war is patently unjust when:

1. Long-term diminishment or destruction of the quality of life for local non-combatants is certain.

"Precision" bombing of water supplies and electrical sources, massive ecological damage and saturation bombardment of an area are not military maneuvers. They are acts of genocide masked as "collateral damage" and aimed at women, children and other defenseless civilians. In Iraq, the UN report stated that "the recent conflict has wrought near-apocalyptic results upon the infrastructure of what had been until January 1991 a rather highly urbanized and mechanized society." UN observers went even further in a March 1991 statement, calling for an immediate end to the embargo on imports of food and other supplies to prevent "epidemic and famine." Nine months after the document was written and released, despite the fact that we chose war rather than the slower process of boycott, the embargoes were still in place, the babies were still dying and the country had lapsed into a grey blur and agonized silence on US television. George Bush and Saddam Hussein had stared each other down in the middle of an international road at high noon, the streets behind them filled with the corpses of the people who had really suffered in a war that clarified nothing and solved less.

2. Long-term financial, economic and political sanctions have not been applied.

In a world where countries are inextricably linked through financial, commercial and political networks there is no country whose borders are not vulnerable to international sanction. To say that a nation must be invaded to control it is unadulterated fantasy. The Soviet Union is clear proof of the effect of marginalization in the family of nations. South Africa began, finally, to moderate its apartheid policy after embargoes were intractably in place—and we never so much as threatened to invade it though its destruction of peoples has been far more massive and far more serious than Iraq's incursion into Kuwait. Then why don't we use commercial sanctions more often? The answer is equally obvious: The problem with economic sanctions is that they take patience and they take courage on the part of people who are normally least inconvenienced by conflict.

The fact is that embargoes of whatever kind hurt the people who profit most from wars—bankers, businessmen and politicians—rather than young soldiers, old reservists and displaced families. It is so much more acceptable to the business community of a country to get a contract or a give a loan to rebuild a nation after a swift war than it is to cut back on the exports and diminish profit margins during the period it will take to discipline a nation by embargo. Preliminary estimates of the cost of rebuilding Kuwait, for instance, are accepted to be in the range of $40 billion dollars, most of which will come to businesses in the United States. It is so much easier in situations like this to be patriotic with the lives of young soldiers than it is to risk the negative reaction of an entire nation to the monetary inconveniences caused by the moral stance they say they want to see an army exert.

3. The negative effects of the combat exceed the negative effects of the original offense.

Proportionality, a standard element of the just war theory, may well be its most ignored aspect and its most needed dimension. While the US military in Iraq proclaimed the success of allied attacks, it failed to report the wholesale devastation of a region that would suffer far more from being liberated than Kuwait ever did from invasion. Civilian life and propery were not in fact saved, though the TV screens touted surgical bombings of military targets.

The question, of course, is whether or not the cure a war brings will not be worse than the disease it purports to cure. Surely the destruction of an entire area of Panama City was more devastating to the innocent of the city than the shady financial machinations of one more dishonest leader. Certainly the defoliation of Vietnam was more destructive to the future of the country than a change of political philosophy would have been in an area that has, over time, outlived dynasty after dynasty. Without doubt, the 200,000 deaths, the ecological devastation of the region, the long-term suffering of the civilian population exacted of Iraq in retaliation for the annexation of Kuwait was clearly disproportionate destruction in the name of justice. To tolerate the routine blurring of the civilian and the military to such a degree is to recast the entire nature of war. Far more innocent people, for instance, were killed in the process of liberating Kuwait, the Greenpeace report confirms, than were killed in the course of its occupation.

That situations such as invasion, occupation, or forced annexation not only deserve to be addressed but demand the response of the international community is not here in question. What is in question is whether or not war as we wage it now can possibly be the best way to deal with the situation and whether the traditional just war theory is adequate to make that determination in a high tech world. In a climate where a pope argues in a letter to the leaders of both nations involved that "even though an unjust situation might be momentarily met, the consequences that would possibly derive from a war would be devastating and tragic" and Raphael I Bidawid, the Chaldean patriarch in Baghdad, claims at the same time that Baghdad had a "just cause," just cause is clearly no longer justification for war.

4. The justice of the initiating situation is open to question

by fair-minded and knowledgeable people.

Legitimate national questions deserve honest international review. Germany made repeated attempts to question the war reparation process that had been imposed on them after World War I but deprived them of the resource-rich Ruhr Valley which would have made reparation payments possible. The rehabilitation of the country was made virtually impossible and the nation was brought to the verge of economic collapse. But the questions were ignored. As a result, Germany became ripe for demagoguery and Hitler was able to rally the country to invade other territories in order to recover the security that had been lost. In our own time, Saddam Hussein complained repeatedly that Kuwait was siphoning oil from Iraq's Rumaili oil fields. The charge was a plausible one and one that was confirmed by reputable news organizations around the world. The claims were suppressed from public view and dismissed without review by the very governments that would lead the invasion to free Kuwait from Iraqi annexation and exact terms of unconditional surrender.

The fact is that as the world becomes more and more inextricably linked, more and more issues are going to demand interpretation and resolution. When the questions are legitimate ones, all-out technological warfare is surely unjust.

5. The issues have not been submitted to an international body for evaluation and recommendation.

Wars between nations now affect and threaten the entire globe. Nuclear proliferation and the arms bazaar in high technology weaponry make even the smallest of nations potentially earth shattering. No single nation can any longer be trusted with the management of such a chain reaction. For any country, then, to launch war, however holy the reasons, without the approval of the entire world community, is to make rogues of both nations. To assume that any cause, any rules of combat can possibly make a situation of that magnitude moral is to ignore the very fabric of humankind. The role of the United Nations in El Salvador, Yugoslavia and Iraq is a hopeful sign. It is yet, however, to be considered to have moral imperative.

6. The combat has not been directed by an international body who is responsible both for the conduct and the resolution of hostilities.

Wars fought by an individual nation will be fought for the good of that nation alone. Treaties imposed by one nation will be designed to favor the winning nation, not the world community. Technology unleashed by one nation will be released with little or no thought of its ecological effect on the globe in general. Yet, war is clearly no longer a private matter. To make it so is to proceed from unjust principles from the outset. When the United Nations handed the conduct of the Gulf War over to the United States, it ceded its role as just judge of what was right and what was necessary. For all practical purposes, it made what may indeed have been a universal issue into a private contest fought—and won—on US terms, a factor that biases both the causes and the results of the war.

7. The nations that are offended by the action are the nations who supplied the arms that made the action possible.

According to James Adams, Associate Editor of *The Sunday Times* of London, in his book, *Engines of War: Merchants of Death and the New Arms Race*, the arms business is a $50 billion annual business that profits both governments and black marketers. To arm a country and then to punish that country for using the weapons for their own ends, as the United States did Iraq, is at least morally schizophrenic. Iraq took Kuwait with the help of US armaments. For the United States to deplore the use of them in a situation that was at least questionable begs for explanation.

The gruesome truth is that, given the modern breakdown between the military and the civilian arenas in the time of war, we can no longer simply assume that justice lies with the winners of a conflict, the people who tell the story of why they did what they did and how they did it after the smoke has cleared. We must begin to see war in terms of its effects on the innocent and the environment as well as through the filter of abstract causes. In a period when international communication blackout, financial control, universal trade and economic boycott are coins of the realm, there is no need for war. There is need for patience, yes, while we wait for natural forces to do what armed force cannot. There is need for political will in the place of military force. There is need for consistency. There is need for respect for life. There is need for a higher level of human development. The Chinese say, "Those who strike another admit that their ideas have run out."

"Impossible," people say. "Unrealistic," they say. "War is inevitable. War is natural." But that's what people said about slavery and monarchy and poverty, as well, until creative minorities changed it all. Ted Koppel, host of ABC's "Nightline" warned, "We are imposing on our minds the same burdens that we have inflicted on our stomachs, precooked ideas designed to appeal to the largest number of people at the lowest possible price: McThought." It is time for new ideas.

It is the measure of the things to which we give our allegiance that is the measure of ourselves. But we have given allegiance to the worst in us, to the notion that what is bad cannot be better.

It is time to remember that the just war theory is just that. It is a theory which, at the very least, is poorly applied or which, given the nature of modern warfare, is clearly inadequate. George Bernard Shaw taught that reasonable people adapt themselves to the world and that unreasonable ones persist in trying to adapt the world to themselves. "Therefore," he wrote, "all progress depends on the unreasonable." We need new ideas about conflict resolution. The old ideas are destroying us. Worse, perhaps, they are measuring the reach of us as human, human beings. It is time to stop temporizing with the intolerable. It is time to become unreasonable about war.

Contemplation

Contemplation, Everyone?

As a young sister, I remember working very hard at prayer. I prepared and prepared for prayer. At that time, our prayer was in Latin. While I wasn't all that bad at Latin, no one really wrestles with the nuances of the spiritual life in another language let alone a dead one. So, I prepared in English as well. Yet, even though my preparation improved, I couldn't see that anything was happening in my life. I didn't feel closer to God or more aware of God's presence.

Then in the early 1960s I was given a copy of *Abandonment to Divine Providence* by Jean-Pierre De Caussade. He added an element that had been missing for me. It was the concept of the sacrament of the present moment, the notion that what is now is where God is for me now.

The awareness of God's presence had become my greatest value. After that, I began to see that we are steeped in God. But our awareness of this is so limited. I think that's true because we have been trained to pray, instead of being trained in prayer.

When you are trained to pray, you can find yourself in a phenomenal amount of formulas, and the pre-Vatican II church abounded in them. These formulas should have been aids to prayer, but often they became ends in themselves: for example, the nine first Fridays, the so-many Saturdays, the so-many decades of the rosary. These are the things I'm thinking of when I say we were trained to pray. It was a very product-oriented method.

Being trained in prayer, on the other hand, can lead to contemplation. Its starting point is the realization that potentially everyone is a contemplative. Contemplation is there for the taking. All you have to do is give yourself over to it. That means you give yourself not to the prayer, or to the prayer formula, but rather to something beyond the prayer, and that something, of course, is Someone, God.

Contemplatives are people whose consciousness of God permeates their entire lives. Their awareness of God's presence magnetizes them and directs them beyond everything else, beyond all other values. Contemplatives are aware that God creates them, sustains them, and challenges them. As a result, all other values and agendas fall away. I don't mean contemplatives find no value in other things—for example, in a career, or money, or achievement. These things, however, never become their greatest value. The awareness of God's presence remains the greatest value.

In essence, according to all the great mystics, contemplation is, and I think continues to be, this consciousness of living steeped in God, of being surrounded by God, of being directed by God, of being in the presence of God, of learning to see life through the eyes of God, of being aware of God's love, action and challenge.

The desert mothers and fathers said that *contemplatio* was best accomplished through manual labor. The ancient literature tells lots of stories about the work that was done by contemplatives—basket weaving, for example, is frequently mentioned.

The link between work and contemplation is very interesting. The desert fathers and mothers were saying contemplation is not idleness. Further, it's not concentration on something else. So who is better for the contemplative life than the person who is working, but not totally caught up in the things he or she is working with? For a person with this approach, work or being busy can become a contemplative act, can be the occasion for fostering the awareness of God's presence.

Many people, I think, sense this. They seem to know intuitively that growing a garden, or painting the house, or raking the leaves are good things to do. Good things happen to people when they are doing such tasks. They use them as a vehicle for bringing their lives to wholeness. That's contemplative. That's coming to awareness. That's giving yourself a chance to see yourself as you are. That's a way of giving yourself a chance to relate your own story to the Jesus story. That's a time you can simply be in the presence of God, and be renewed and revived by that presence. But you have to make time and space for it. Once you make it a practice, it has a way of overflowing even into moments that are consciously being spent reading, working through problems, organizing, administering. Sometimes there are only flashes of awareness, but there is a consistent relationship, a consistent consciousness. I don't think you can deal anyone out of that.

I don't think anyone can live contemplatively without discipline, and that includes your local monk or nun. So, if I am going to live as a contemplative in the suburbs, I am going to have to structure my life, just as a monk or nun must structure his or her life. In both cases, the structure, while it will be different in detail, must be such that it provides regular nourishment for the contemplative dimension of life. This includes regular *lectio*, or spiritual reading, to undergird it and to challenge the way I am living.

People living in the suburbs, and in our society generally, can make choices about the way they live, though most of them don't see that, because they are conditioned to be on the go all the time, usually at someone else's behest, from early in the morning till late at night.

Imagine for a moment what America would look like, imagine the degree of serenity we'd have, if lay people had something comparable to the daily schedule of the cloistered life. It provides scheduled time for prayer, work and recreation.

Of course such a schedule wouldn't look the way mine does as a Benedictine, but it would have the same components—time for work, time for family and community, time for the Christian community, time for private scripture reading and reflection. Out of that would come a whole new rhythm of life, a whole new way of seeing the relative importance of various parts of one's life. It could provide the discipline, the structure, to help people make the awareness of the presence of God the greatest value in life.

Some might say this is an unreal expectation in this whirlwind world, but it might be easier than ever before because we have advantages not available in an earlier age. A married woman with children who works outside the home and commutes to work, for example, might not do her *lectio*, spiritual reading, with a book. Instead, she might get the spiritual nourishment provided by *lectio* through listening to a tape while commuting to work or working around the house. This might mean cutting out listening to hard rock or watching "Days of Our Lives." But becoming a contemplative does involve discipline as well as desire.

And what about her job? As I've already pointed out, work is not necessarily an impediment to contemplation. We all have to work. St. Benedict knew that. There's a marvelous chapter in the Rule saying, in effect, when you have to get the harvest in, you have to get the harvest in. So pray in the fields! Don't tell me, he's saying, that you left the wheat out in the rain because you had to be home at a certain time to pray, to contemplate. This, the wheat, is what must be attended to now. Do it. This is your contemplation.

When I was a young sister, prayer was my distraction. I couldn't imagine why the prioress couldn't understand there were more important things to do than pray. But after some time of the discipline, prayer became the refreshment, became the thing I couldn't live without.

Contemplation was no longer a burden. It gave meaning to everything else I was doing, no matter how busy I was. It became my center. It gave me direction. It brought me home. I began to see all of my "good works" in relationship to my awareness of the presence of God. This made these "good works" relative. They were no longer my ultimate value. A woman living in the suburbs can do the same with her "good works."

To be sure, you must nourish your awareness of God's presence in your life and in the world. But eventually, it won't be a burden, it won't be an exercise. It *is*. This awareness of God's presence will always be the filter through which you think and act and pray. This presence will always stand between you and over you and around you in everything you are doing.

Tradition

The Justice Lessons
Jesus Grew Up On

There's an ancient story that bears retelling, perhaps, in an age of discrimination, refugees, planned destruction of the planet, government lies and the industrialized slavery of the Third World.

Once upon a time, the story goes, a disciple said to the elder, "Holy One, I have a great spiritual question to ask. Is there life after death?" And the Holy One answered: "Ah, that is an interesting question but it is not the greatest of spiritual questions. The greatest of spiritual questions is, Is there life before death?"

A second imperative from scripture is related to the first. The Book of Proverbs teaches: "Lead a child up in the way they must go and when they are old they will not depart from the way."

Jesus was devoted to life before death and Jesus was formed in it from childhood. If we want life before death, we will have to be developed in the same way.

Most of the Catholics of my generation were formed in the catechism; religion was reduced to absolutes and laws, to lists of sins and lists of Holy Days of Obligation, to theological formulas and personal devotions, to legalism and pietism. Religion was a private matter; individualism was the high priest of the New World and "the white man's burden" was the bedrock of foreign policy.

No wonder we grew up looking so different from the Jesus who said, "Feed my sheep," and the Jesus who rose to return, not to Jerusalem—the center of power—but to Galilee, the backwater of Israel where the poor and the outcast, the illiterate and the unwanted, the simple and the unsophisticated were waiting for deliverance. Jesus, you see, was not raised on the catechism. Jesus was raised on the psalms.

Sung for centuries, the psalms have captured the spiritual wisdom and insights of one generation after another. They sing of praise and fear and faith and final victory. They sing all the human emotions to God. They talk to God. They scour the world for answers to the unanswerable. They ring across time with the human memory of the fidelity of God and the soul searching of humanity and the highest aspirations and the deepest pain of the human soul. They sing of a theology of human life that transcends national boundaries and personal privatism and private profitism. They sing of the whole human race united in the God who is life. They sing of a people who sin as a people and are saved as a people and sigh for God as a people and see God everywhere. The psalms are a crash course in justice, not a compendium of laws. The psalms called Jesus beyond Judaism and stretch us still beyond ourselves.

It is impossible to pray the psalms and settle for parochialism. It is inconceivable to pray the psalms and foster national chauvinism. It is unthinkable to pray the psalms and wallow in a theology of domination that gives some of us the right to misuse the rest of us in the name of capitalism or communism or clericalism or sexism or racism or arrogance.

And Jesus was aware of that because Jesus prayed the psalms as a way of life.

What did Jesus learn in the psalms that we theologize about, perhaps, but take more as questions than as answers?

Jesus learned that the poor are heard. "You listen to the needy and the oppressed," Psalm 69 declares. "When the poor cry to me

I will hear them," Psalm 34 insists. It is a dire warning for those with ears to hear. The psalms do not say that the poor will be miraculously saved. Oh, no. The psalms simply promise that the poor will be heard. And remembered presumably. And vindicated in the end. Like Lazarus with Dives.

The psalms imply quite forthrightly that though you and I may not hear the poor, God will. Eventually. When it counts. And you and I who do not hear them and stoop down to them and reach out to them and stand up for them will ourselves go unheard on the side of God's deaf ear.

And so Jesus, formed in the psalms, heard the poor on the Sabbath and in the temple and at the tables of the rich.

The question for our time is whether or not we, too, speak for the poor of our worlds—for the blacks who are being deprived of their culture in the name of Catholicism while Anglos and Europeans have it aplenty, for the women who are being told that Jesus' message to them is, "Don't follow me," for the theologians who are attempting to ask new questions so that the gospel can be relevant to a new age, and for the poor of the world in Harlem and South Africa and Central America who are left out of a capitalist equation in which weakness is not acceptable and people are expendable.

Jesus learned in the psalms that the world is a cosmic reality, not a local and nationalistic preserve of the chosen few. "The creator loves all the children of earth and shapes the hearts of each," Psalm 33 reminds us. God's blessing rains on all, in other words. "God touches all in the heavens and on earth," Jesus was constantly reminded. "Everything is full of sacred presence," he heard in Psalm 103. In the face of the unseeing and the uncaring, Jesus learned that the planet is not ours for the exploiting. The universe is not ours for the controlling. The people are not ours for the enslaving. God gives good and wants good for everyone.

Jesus, it is clear, blessed Jew and non-Jew alike, the centurion and the Samaritan, the woman as well as the man, the world's unjust as well as the just. In God, the psalms say to a world of debutante balls and closed clubs and "undeveloped" peoples, there are simply no standards, no status qualifications, no people with whom we associate in contrast to those with whom we do not, no nations less bright, less human, less deserving of the fruits of humankind than we are.

Yet we take our factories into the Third World and decide the level at which those people may live. Indeed, we export our industries but not our wage scales or our pension plans or our labor standards or our health benefits and say that we have done a good thing. "Where would those people be without our industry?" we argue and buy caftans in the Philippines for $7.00 each and sell them in Florida for $70.00 apiece. And we pride ourselves on the fact that we ended the slavery system that provided our domestic labor with a house and a family network so that today we can pay slave wages and not be required to provide the house and food for the slave family. It is a spirituality that is far removed from the psalms that cried out for justice to the widow, the orphan and the foreigner, for recognition of the sacred presence in all.

What Jesus learned in Psalm 145 is that God is the God of all. "All creatures look to you with hope," Jesus learned to pray, "and you sustain them in their need. You are generous to all creation, nourishing all who live." And Jesus taught Samaritans and cured pagans and talked to Romans and taught women, whom Jews disdained in the public arena, some very public things. It was to women, in fact, that Jesus first taught the fact that he was the Messiah and that he was risen from the dead.

Discrimination in the name of religion, in other words, is a heinous thing. A crusade against Arabs and a holocaust of Jews has no place in the lives of a psalmic people. The obliteration of the Romans and the neglect of the Samaritans has no rank in the mind of those who have begun to see the world through the filter of the psalms. The nuclear disintegration of the planet is simply unthinkable to a psalmic people. The exploitation of the globe is lunatic to a psalmic people. The feminization of poverty is unimaginable to a psalmic people. The denigration and disen franchisement and theological erasure of women is simply unac- ceptable to a people who pray the psalms and understand the psalms and grow in the spirituality of the psalms.

"Vengeance is mine; I shall repay," Jesus learned from the psalms. "The power of the wicked shall be broken. God takes care of the just," Jesus breathed over and over again in Psalm 37. And surely the concept was comforting when he faced the hostile rabbis and the scornful soldiers and the manipulated witnesses. But in a search for false peace, we have perhaps forgotten the energy that comes from knowing holy anger and leaving the results to God.

There have been movements, even in the monastic prayer tradition, that are based squarely in the center of the psalms, to eliminate what have come to be called the "Cursing Psalms." "What place does cursing have in prayer?" the purists argue. But perhaps the better question is, Where else shall we take our curses than to prayer where we acknowledge at the time of our deepest pain that punishment does not belong to us, that God is the God of justice? How else do we explain that Jesus went "like a lamb to slaughter," not without struggle, but without meanness, because Jesus knew that whatever the price of his own commitment, God would in the end do it justice? How else do we account for the fact that Jesus does not call down the hosts of heaven even in his own behalf or allow Peter to take up the sword? How else do we explain the fact that Jesus saw sin and did not punish it, saw pain and did not condone it, saw truth and did not flinch from it?

But we revel in those who take justice into their own hands and take preeminence to ourselves and take racism as the will of God and take sexism as natural. Abraham Lincoln pointed out to those who prayed that the North would win the Civil War that it did not matter whether or not God was on our side but what mattered was simply whether or not we were on God's side. That was a psalmic mentality far removed from a period of messianic Americanism. We can invade a country and displace its people and gerrymander its government in the name of our own justice. We can suspend the principles of the Constitution as long as we are not on American territory, the Supreme Court has ruled. We can, apparently, usurp and exploit and undermine for our own brand of truth and justice as long as it is in the interest of the USA, no matter who is hurt or who is forgotten or who is destroyed and call ourselves a religious people and everyone else pagan. But that is not the psalmic mentality of Jesus to whom Samaritans are worth saving and women are worth raising from the dead and Romans are worth obeying.

"Uphold my cause, O God, for I walk in integrity. I trust in you. I shall stand firm," Jesus prayed in Psalm 26. Trust, indeed, became the cornerstone of a Jesus who was not received by those to whom he was sent and rejected by those whom he had healed and misunderstood by those to whom he had explained himself. Trust became what drove him on and kept him certain in the face of confusion and failure and disinterest. It is trust that we, too, must learn if our own lives are to have purpose and constancy in the midst of fatigue. How does anyone go on in the peace movement or the woman's issue or the justice questions who does not trust that a better heart than the hearts that rule the systems and write the laws and share the wealth will ultimately gain the day? The Jesus who trusted all the way to Calvary is the Jesus who asks us to trust as well. But trust is not a virtue until there is reason to despair. This psalmic people who knew slavery and exile and siege and destruction taught the world to trust. And in Jesus came the clearest sign of it.

Indeed the mind of Jesus has been formed very differently from ours. Obviously, the psalms outdo the boundaries of the catechism and the provincialism of a nation and the narrowness of bigots.

"Let those who hope in you not be put to shame through me, God of Hosts," Jesus prayed in Psalm 69.

"Let not those who seek you be dismayed through me, God of Israel," Jesus learned. No one, in other words, should see in us anything that makes them doubt the authenticity of the Christian revelation, that God lives in us. People should be able to see in us what our God is like. Whatever we do, we do as sign to others of the continuing presence of a caring, courageous Christ. That's what being Christian is all about. That's what it is to be formed in the psalms, as Jesus was.

Advocacy, creationism, universalism, justice, trust and witness is what Jesus learned in the psalms and lived when he cured on the Sabbath and modeled when he touched the doubly polluted corpse of the woman and witnessed to when he listened to the poor and risked when he disputed with the rabbis in the temple. It is, to this day, the legacy of the psalms. Maybe that's why a domesticated people are less inclined to pray them now.

Prayer, of course, is not meant to be a magic act that cajoles and coaxes God to turn life into a Disneyland of religion. Prayer is not meant to change the world; prayer is meant to change us so that we will then change the world.

Jesus, clearly, had learned to pray. The question for our time is, Have we? We know how to worry, we know how to beg, we know how to fantasize in prayer, we know how to make prayer an escape. But we will not be praying until we have become immersed in the mind and presence of God, as Jesus was, until we have come to see God everywhere, in everyone, until we have come to listen to the poor, until we have come to work as God would work in this world, until we have come to give our wrath over to the wrath of God, until we have come to trust and trust and trust that somehow, someday what must happen will happen because we have added our part to it.

As he walks the dry and dusty roads of Galilee with the poor and unsophisticated, we see how the psalms have formed Jesus. As he debates the doctrines of law with the doctors of the church who have shaped the possibilities of God to themselves, we see how the psalms have formed Jesus. As he gives people more care and attention than he does institutions, we see how the psalms have formed Jesus. As we see his non-denominationalism, his awareness of God everywhere, in everyone, we see how the psalms have formed Jesus.

The question is, then, What is forming us? When the papers point out that we are deporting the poor from the richest nation in the world, we must ask what is forming us. When we maximize our profits at the expense of others, we must ask what is forming us. When we name some peoples expendable or ignorable, or uneducable, we must ask what is forming us. When we swallow our holy angers for the sake of a plastic peace or strike out to destroy what is not yet like us, we must ask what is forming us. When we forget that there is injustice in the world because the just do nothing about it, we must ask what is forming us. When we despair of God's grace or God's presence or God's consuming and ultimate justice, we must ask what adolescent, magical, superficial and fanciful notions of God are forming us.

Jesus pronounced his own formation directly. "I have come that they may have life and have it more abundantly," he declared. "The great spiritual question," the Holy One said, "is not whether or not there is life after death. The great spiritual question is whether or not there is life before death."

Those are the fruits of real spiritual formation. To have life and to give life, now and overflowing. Those are the ideas that formed Jesus and those are the convictions, if we are ever to be truly Christian, that must someday form us.

Sabbath

Sins of the '90s:
The Last Sabbath

The 20th century may, when the long view of history makes a final assessment, rank as one of the crossover moments in the development of the human race. Two world wars, the institutionalized holocaust of an entire people, the nuclearization of the globe, the dawn of organ transplants, the advent of scientific birth control, the cloning of animals, the wholesale raping of natural resources and the emergence of the Internet all signal a period of massive change, a reshaping of the human economy. Life-altering situations such as these constitute the before and after moments of a watershed culture. The apex of the Enlightenment ideal for many, they are, at the same time, perceived by others as the ultimate low point of classical philosophy. From one perspective or another, they denote science run rampant or traditional theology under siege. Out of them have come some of the best, and some of the worst, moments in human history.

Indeed, the century has brought us both great threat and great possibility. Interestingly enough, though each of these historical moments, and many other moments, as well, depending on who's naming them, may certainly figure in somebody's catalogue of sins or someone else's catechism of progress, the mere branding of these elements and others like them as either good or bad does not necessarily testify to any of them morally. It takes a great deal more than either public approval or personal denouncement to mark anything as certainly moral, amoral or immoral. It takes reflection. It takes care. It takes criteria to evaluate a thing. It takes reflection and soul. It takes exactly what we may in our time now be missing most: the spirit of Sabbath. One of the cardinal sins of the 1990s may well be the loss of Sabbath.

Play we know about and make it big business. Leisure we are committed as a culture to pursuing. The concept of Sabbath, however, simply escapes the modern mind. Despite the fact that the idea of Sabbath is the oldest in the Judeo-Christian tradition, it is, in a culture of cars and planes, of 24 hour-a-day shopping malls and seven-day-a-week services, the lost art of the twentieth century.

Scholars of the Talmud tell us that the reason God created Sabbath was not because God needed rest but in order to model rest, to sanctify rest, to demand rest of us so that by regularly resting in God we could ourselves become new people. Sabbath, the tradition says, crowns life with four dimensions.

In the first place, thanks to Sabbath, everyone in the society is equal at least one day a week. On the Sabbath, both rich and poor have the right to live a privileged life exempt from drudgery. Secondly, Sabbath makes the whole world free. The upper class puts down its burden of administration. The lower class, the slaves, lives free from the demand to take orders. The third gift of Sabbath, the rabbis teach us, is the foretaste of heaven that comes with resting in God, refreshing family life and internalizing the Word that nourishes our souls for the rest of the week. The fourth blessing of the Sabbath comes from taking the time to consider the purpose of life, to determine if we can say with the Creator about our own work in the world, "That's good." The product I make enhances life and "That's good." The wages I pay enable life and "That's good." The decisions I make bring justice to life and "That's good."

Sabbath, in other words, is meant to enrich life, to measure life, to bring reflection to life, to engender life with soul.

Sabbath is for resting in the God of life and bringing more to life ourselves as a result. Sabbath stays us in mid-course and gives us the opportunity to begin again, week after week after week. If one-seventh of every life is devoted to rest, then we have been given 52 days a year, or over 3,500 days in 70 years, or approximately ten years of Sabbath or rest or reflection in a lifetime—all designed to be used to determine the meaning and substance, the purpose and direction of our lives. Sabbath should be those time-out days when we allow ourselves to look at life in fresh and penetrating ways. Sabbath calls us to worship what deserves to be worshipped and to dismiss from the center of our souls what does not.

But our society has found other things to worship on the Sabbath. We have come to worship consumerism by turning Sundays into some of the biggest shopping days of the year. We have come to worship freedom from family, freedom from worship, freedom from the self. Thinking has become the last thing in the world we want to do on the Sabbath. We have turned thought into human vegetation and called it rest. We have made a desert of the soul and called it re-creation. We have substituted play and leisure for soul-searching and beauty, for intimacy and awareness of the larger things in life. We have created a culture that turns the Sabbath into a race for escape, a passion for things, a collection of distractions, a paean to emptiness.

Indeed, we are a long, long way from Sabbath and so near, so very near, to social dissipation as a result.

We don't stop to think much about anything anymore. We don't stop at all, in fact. Our generation has learned to "multitask," to "manage" our time. We open our mail while we talk on the telephone. We correct papers or shift computer files while we watch television. We take the kids to play in the park while we sit in the car to finish writing this month's report. We work every day of the week and twice as much on the Sabbath. It's become catch-up time instead of reflection time. We have lost a sense of awareness, of attention, of what the monastics call "mindfulness." No wonder we can come to the brink of human cloning and hardly notice. No wonder we can watch the oppression of half the human race and take it for granted. No wonder we can watch the total unraveling of life in every arena and find little or no time to participate in the public debates that ought to underlie the creation of social consensus before we find ourselves inheriting what we did not desire, acceding to what we cannot morally sustain, bequeathing what we dare not countenance.

When Yahweh created the Sabbath, the specter of thoughtlessness was created, as well. Having created the opportunity for awareness, the opportunity for the oblivious was created as well. We unleashed nuclear weapons upon the world and failed to think about the moral implications of that, both then and now. We clawed our way through the rain forests and failed to consider as a people the long-range implications of that for generations to come. We lost a sense of Sabbath and took no notice as a culture of the starvation of soul, the loss of intimacy and the exhaustion of mind that derived from depriving ourselves of reflection. We turned Sundays into weekdays and wonder what happened to neighbors and nature and our nervous systems.

We multi-task. We buy. We run from ourselves at increasingly greater speeds. Clearly, the sin is not in the science, in the profit, in the play. The sin lies in the loss of the Sabbath mind, the regularly recurring awareness that science and money and play are merely elements of life, not its essence.

The proverb reads, "Now people exploit people. But after the revolution, it will be just the opposite." Without the reawakening of the Sabbath mind, there is no doubt.

Worship

Liturgy: To Comfort or Liberate

The Hasidim tell us two things about the practice of faith that may teach more about liturgy than all the theory in all the textbooks of the world. The first is a story. Once upon a time, the rabbis say, Abraham wished to enable humankind to worship God well and so he instituted the morning service. But Satan conspired against this and filled it with distracting thoughts. So Isaac said, "I will institute a briefer service through which humankind may perhaps be able to pray with greater concentration." But prayer time went rampant nevertheless. And this liturgy, too, proved of no avail.

So Jacob then said, "I will proclaim a voluntary evening service; then, perhaps, Satan will not trouble to interrupt what people may choose not to read." But this, too, was unsuccessful. The best of worshippers failed often to focus entirely on God.

So Ari said, "I will institute the practice of silent meditations where there are no words to conjure up other thoughts and so cannot be corrupted by the mundane." But that didn't work either.

Finally, the Baal Shem Tov said, "Let pious people who cannot pray prayers properly recite aloud choice sayings and good stories and endow those things with whatever holy meaning they may have for them." So then, the rabbis said, Satan could not enter there again.

The point of the rabbis' teaching is clear: The stuff of holiness is not necessarily holy stuff. Doing holy things does not necessarily take us to God. But, whatever takes us to God, whatever excites us, engages us, affects our souls—whatever has meaning for us today, is holy-making for us.

The second great liturgical insight of the rabbinic masters is this one, perhaps. The Talmud says, "God is not nice; God is not an uncle; God is an earthquake."

The question for us, then, is no less the question of Abraham and Isaac, of Jacob and Ari, and of pastoral ministers everywhere and always, What is the nature of prayer today? Is its purpose to comfort us in an uncomfortable world or to challenge us in a complacent one? And whatever it is, How shall we enable it?

What is the role of liturgy today—to comfort the challenged in an oppressive world or to liberate the oppressed in an oppressing world—and how shall we know? And how shall we achieve it? The world is full of Christian churches but the world is also full of the obscenely poor. How shall we explain that? And what does it have to do with being a pastoral minister?

The answer, I believe, is that it has everything to do with being a pastoral minister. The answer, I believe, is that it is the only thing that has anything to do with really being a pastoral minister.

It is an unusually portentous time for the church, not because there are problems—the church has always known problems, problems of heresy, problems of faith, problems of nepotism, problems of simony. Problems that ate at its very core, at its structures and dogmas, its clergy and popes, its powerful and its power. This time, our time, is most portentous of all, however, because the problems are very different now.

This time the church faces questions of consequence and credibility, of focus and role, as in few other periods in modern history, excepting, perhaps, the periods of the Reformation and the Enlightenment. The problems of these times weigh heavier for the church if for no other reason than the fact that global communication and computer technology make any problems more precipitous. Now, things once remote are universally present—a priest shortage in Africa is a problem for the whole church; things once speculative are now immediate—genetic research in the US is now both promise and threat to the whole world. Now everyone once totally separate, are close confederates on the same delicate universe, the same global neighborhood, the same tender earth—grazing herds for US fast food chains in Brazilian rain forests choke off the lungs of the world. Clearly, the stuff of holy stuff has changed.

As a result, religion, like everything else in life and everything else in life despite religion, finds itself too often awash in more questions than answers, in more doubt than certainty, in more misgiving than conviction. It is in a world such as this that pastoral ministers do their ministry, and perform their pastoring—not under the auspices of "Christendom," not in the secure shadow of established chants, not under the classical cosmology of Michaelangelo, not through the mechanical syllogisms of scholasticism, but more in the throes of disorientation, more in the face of reactionary conservatism, more under the scrutiny of a wailing, wondering world than under either the impulse of pious fear or the assurances of absolutism.

Let there be no doubt about it, never in our lifetimes have we needed good pastoral ministers more than we do now. The question of the role of liturgy—to comfort or to liberate—is not an academic one any longer. The thinkers want to know if religion thinks. The oppressed want to know if religion cares. The children want to know if religion has anything whatsoever to say about how a new world, their world, grows up.

There are more than enough reasons—social, cultural, theological and global—to wrestle with the subject daily.

First, there has been a major cultural shift in the relationship between religion and life. Modern social science is full of the struggle. Gallup polls in the early 1990s reported that church attendance held steady in the US but that the notion that religion is an important factor in life has declined from 75% in 1952 to less than 50% in 1990.

The military, Gallup tells us, has replaced the church for the first time in polling history as the nation's most trusted institution and half the population says that religion is losing its influence on American life. Clearly, this is a public that goes to church and finds no answers. This is a public that is seeking but says that we don't show the way.

According to *Faith and Ferment*, an interdisciplinary study of contemporary Christian belief sponsored by the Ecumenical and Cultural Research Center at St. John's University, MN, people reported that they saw little or no relationship between what they heard from the church and what they were faced with in life. They saw little or no relationship between religion and ecology. So much for the Garden of Eden.

They saw little or no relationship between business ethics and religion. So much for the cleansing of the temple. They saw little or no relationship between the teachings of Christianity and their standard of living. So much for the rich young man. They saw little or no relationship between religion and their ideas on war. So much for Peter and his sword, a host of angels and a crucifixion. "The churches are unclear," they said. Indeed, the culture is crying out for pastoring.

There has been a theological shift: While faith built on mystery has flourished, belief built on myth has frazzled. Old hierarchical structures have crumbled. "Because we said so," is no longer a basis for belief. Old explanations have been found wanting; medieval mindsets with their emphasis on flat worlds and private pieties have gone the way of the medieval world. Theology itself has been challenged by itself, all inquisitions to the contrary, all silencings with resounding disregard, all final discussions eternally reopened in the living rooms, discussion groups, universities and families of the world—reopened everywhere, in fact, except in the church itself.

Liberation theology, planetary theology, feminist theology,

have brought the questions of the world to the door step of the church, its pain to the tabernacles, the inconsistencies, the oppressions, of the teaching itself to the highest levels of the Vatican. They have brought life to dead wood. Patriarchy died with feminism; clericalism died with the document on the laity; ecclesiastical imperialism died with ecumenism; ghettoism died with globalism. And any church that sings these things will die with them.

Pastoral ministers cannot simply sing the anthems of an old church and old images in an old world. Pastoral ministers are responsible for defining the meaning, the concerns, the social morality, the theological vision, of a new church in a shifting world. This time, like the Hasidim, we need to find old holiness in new places, all of them extremely profane, some of them profanely extreme. The challenge to liturgy at any time is always great. At such a time as this it is immense, and pastoral ministers will have a great deal to do with the way we as a church make theological choices. And ministerial decisions.

The symbols and songs we sing, the words we pray, the things we pray for shape souls to the size of our spiritual worlds. All the time we prayed our chauvinistic "three Hail Marys for the conversion of Russia," for instance, it never crossed our nuclear minds that our own conversion lurked very much in question. Good pastoral ministers might have saved us decades of militarism.

This time our choices are even greater: This time we must decide whether we as a church shall sing and pray ritual sacrifice or Sabbath meaning, become patriarchal cult or gospel community.

It is simple, of course, to create a cult. Sociologists Richard Offshe and Suzanne Johnson argue that it is not ideology that either creates or maintains a cult. On the contrary. It is the dynamics of the group itself. Cults, sociologists tell us, have five major characteristics:

1. They consist of clear belief systems that justify the totalitarian authority of the leader.

2. Cults are highly controlled and internally authoritarian. The rules are precise and members are punished for breaking them.

3. Cults are dominated by powerful leaders to whom people owe total accountability.

4. Cults defend themselves from influences and personal connections outside the group that might dilute their certainties.

5. Cults maintain adherence to the group by teaching the members that allowing the group to direct their lives will solve their problems and relieve their guilt.

By substituting an unyielding set of religious practices and a strong leadership figure, cults substitute public practices for personal conscience, personal behaviors for public responsibility, personal conformity—public conformity, in fact—for spiritual adulthood, for personal growth.

Doing liturgy for a group such as that is easy. Just build the church around the pastor. Just follow the rules. Just say the words, sing the songs that preserve an insulated society like a hothouse in winter, regardless of what happens to the individual soul, to personal conscience, to human equality, to social justice, then we will clearly have churches. The question is only whether or not we will have the gospel.

We are called to be other Christs—to heal lepers, to confront Pharisees, and, when necessary, even to overturn the tables in the temple. We are called to consort with the poor, to eat with social outcasts, to receive the enemy, with trust and time and touch, even when they are unmarried women on welfare, and young men with AIDS and minorities who are the majorities of the world and who threaten us by wanting back the wealth stolen from them by the West.

In a world like that we are not called to provide a spiritual jacuzzi for the disinterested or pious of the world, we are not called to build satisfied congregations. We are not called to preserve the clerical state. We are called to be church. We are called to be Christian. We are called to bring holy questions to unholy stuff—right in the middle of the Eucharist, right in the middle of the assembly, right in the middle of the comfortable.

We are called to bring into being a church for the *aniwim*, the little ones, the remnant of Israel, who wait and believe and pray and do the word because they have received the host, not receive the host and ignore the word.

Jesus, we know, is really present, Vatican II teaches us, in three places: in the Eucharist, of course, in the Word as well, and in the assembly. Jesus is really present in three places. Not in one. To have a liturgy that does not make the Word present today is empty exercise, not liturgy. To have a liturgy that concentrates on the Eucharistic rite to the exclusion of the presence of Jesus in a Word made alive for today—its questions, its concerns, its moral conundrums, its social outcasts—is to flirt with magic.

To have a liturgy that concentrates on transubstantiation of bread and fails to call for the conversion of people from the pious to the prophetic, to have a liturgy that ignores the sacrifice of Christ in the lives of bleeding people is cult. The fact is that Genesis is clear: We are held responsible for life in this world and it is liturgy that must help us to achieve this spiritual task by confronting us with it and calling us to it.

Liturgy is not to be an escape valve from reality; liturgy is to be reality run amuk in daily life. Liturgy is prophetic vision, prophetic sign, prophetic call to all of us to "go you and do likewise." But without hearing it in the church, how can the church possibly do it?

"Without vision, the people perish," the scripture says. But that is not completely true. It is not true that without vision, the people perish. What is true is that without vision, the people will believe anything at all—will believe that religion is wizardry, will believe that religion is optional, will believe that religion is an avoidance reaction to life; will believe that religion for its own sake is enough; will believe that religion is useless, dead, gone, dried up, pathetic in its feeble-minded impotency at a time of social rage.

"Never pray in a room without windows," the Talmud teaches. Never pray, in other words, without keeping one eye on the world around you. Never pray to escape the world. Pray only to take it in. But how shall we do that? And where shall we go for models of pastoral ministers in a time such as ours, in a time when the issues outside the church door render the church itself suspect? I suggest as the patron saints of pastoral ministers those singers of scriptures whose songs called us to things outside ourselves, beyond ourselves, despite ourselves.

In a church that itself refuses to deal with church-shattering questions of celibacy, the ordination of women, militarism and birth control, take as a patron saint of pastoral ministers Miriam the sister of Moses who was ostracized for criticizing the system but without whom the community, scripture says, could not take another step toward the promised land.

In a world where creation is mocked and creation is scourged, take as a patron saint of pastoral ministers David, the psalmic king, who praised God in all creation, not simply in the Hebrew community.

In a world where women and children die in wars of old men's making, take as patron saint of pastoral ministers the three young men in the fiery furnace whose song of faith maintained their endurance through pain and suffering beyond belief.

In a church where women are denied the right to be so much as spiritual directors to men, take as patron saint of pastoral ministers Anna, the prophetess, who saw in Jesus what others could not see and proclaimed it to the world.

In a world where the richest country in the world makes its money selling weapons to the poorest people in the world, take as patron saint of pastoral ministers Deborah the judge who led the people of Israel to confront their oppressors with nothing but their faith.

In a church that sends to men the letters of apology that it writes to women, and refuses them so much as a pronoun in scripture, and gives women all the responsibilities but few of the rights of the faith, and goes on defining them as a separate species unfit to approach the altar or to act as moral agents, take as patron saint of pastoral ministers Mary, the mother of Jesus, the woman who turned the spirit of God into the body and blood of Jesus, take the woman who knew she was called to be a channel of God's grace whatever lesser truth the men of the place believed, take the woman without whom no man would ever say a Mass.

Center yourselves in Miriam and David, in Anna and the three young men, in Deborah and Mary—sing their songs, pray their prayers, build their church, walk with their God and the church shall be forever safe.

Sing Miriam and David, Anna and the three young men, Deborah and Mary. Sing whatever "choice phrases, whatever fine stories" it takes to wake up our minds, to see what is going on around us, to impel our hearts, to change our souls, to bring God, the earthquake, into our lives.

Conversion

Why I Stay

"It is good to have an end to journey towards," Ursula Le Guin writes, "but it is the journey that matters in the end." The truth of that statement explains, as well as anything, I think, how it is possible, necessary even, for me as a Roman Catholic to stay in a church that is riddled with inconsistencies, closed to discussion about the implications of them, and sympathetic only to invisible women. The fact is that I have come to realize over the years that church is not a place, it is a process. To leave the church may, in fact, be leaving part of the process of my own development. And so, intent on the process of grappling with truth, I stay in it when, for a woman, staying in it is full of pain, frustration, disillusionment and far too often, even humiliation. Both of us, this church and I, have need to grow. The church needs to grow in its understanding of the gospel and I need to grow in my understanding of myself as I strive to live it. It is, in other words, a journey of conversion for both of us.

There is, moreover, a model for the staying that lurks within me, prodding me in hard times to trust my questions, accusing me on dark days of prizing weakness more than truth, consoling me in hard times with the courage of endurance, and inspiring me always to maintain the faith whatever the weakness of the system that heralds it. The images that haunt me are the memories of Jesus contesting with the Pharisees, Jesus weeping over Jerusalem, Jesus teaching in the synagogue and Jesus presiding over the Seder on Holy Thursday. My models are clear: they are Jesus proclaiming his truth whatever the situation, whatever the cost; Jesus grappling with the depression that comes from failure, from rejection; Jesus trusting the truth, living the faith and hoping to the end.

Those are the models that make the rest of the journey—its purpose, its value—clear to me. Staying in the church even when the church has little time for women's presence, takes little notice of women's questions, holds little respect for women's insights, devotes itself to preaching the gospel of equality for women but preserves a male theology and a male system, this demands a purpose far beyond ourselves.

I stay in the church, a restless pilgrim, not because I don't believe what the church has taught me but precisely because I do. I believed when they taught us that God made us equal and Jesus came for us all. I believed in the Jesus they showed me who listened to women and taught theology to women and sent women to teach theology and raised women from the dead. And so today, I believe that the church, if it is ever to be true to that same gospel, must someday do the same—it must commission women as Jesus did the Samaritan woman, listen to women as Jesus did the Caananite women, raise women to new life as Jesus did the daughter of Jairus. I stay in the church because there is nowhere else I know that satisfies in me what the church itself teaches us to seek: a sacramental life that makes all life sacred, a community of faith that celebrates life together, the proclamation of the image of God alive in each of us, the contemplation of truth that makes life meaningful. I know clubs and societies and congregations of deep sincerity who do great good. The problem is that I need sacrament and common faith and a sense of the divine in the core of my humanity as well as I need good talk, good works and good intentions.

I stay in the church because, though the lights have gone out in parts of the house, I know myself to be at home. I realize now with penetrating anger how sexist the church itself really is, whatever its professions of faith in Jesus and love for women. But I also realize that this is the family I was raised in. This is the family that gave me my first images of God, my first feeling of human worth, my first sense of holiness, my first invitation to a goodness measured by more than "success." Just because a family is dysfunctional, as this one is, does not make it less the family. If anything, we must work all the harder to bring all of us to health in it.

I stay in the church because I have the support from other women, from feminist men, from a women's community that enables me to worship with human dignity and a sense of theological inclusion. Otherwise, I do not know how possible it would be to stay. At the same time, because I know my own need for the strength of a conscious and understanding community, I have come to understand and honor those who, lacking that kind of support, choose to leave it. For many, church-going has become more an experience of systemic devaluation than spiritual growth. After years of waiting for change, then, they have chosen to try to find God by themselves rather than being excluded by the community from the common search. These are the women in whom beats a Catholic heart but, like many another abused or belittled woman, they get to the point where, for their mental health, say with pain and still with love, "I will not divorce you but until this changes, I cannot live under the same roof."

I stay in the church for the simple reason that because it has come through so much already, I know it can come through more. This is the church that finally repented the Inquisition, that eventually accepted Galileo, that at length stopped selling relics, and that, in the end, caught up with Luther and at long last embraced an ecumenical movement. Among other things. This is a church that has known sin and regretted it. This is a church that has the potential, the credentials, to understand mine, as well.

I stay in the church, wiser now, less idealistic, more balanced in my hope for instant change, more spiritually mature myself, perhaps. In the first two weeks of my initial trip to Rome in 1972, I was appalled by what I saw there—the pomp, the posturing, the oppressive and arrogant sense of power that seeped out of every office, hung over every meeting, colored every ritual. I was young and intense. I had, I thought, lost my faith. I wanted never to go back there. *"Patientia, patientia,"* an old monastic counseled. "You will come back and you will grow to understand...." The sentence trailed off into irritating nothingness. Understand what? But by the end of the next two weeks and the next fifteen years of meetings there, I came to understand its meaning for myself. I grew to realize that for those whose faith is mature, only God is God. Not the institution. Not the system. Not the history. Not the pope. God is in the church, not in the chancery. The church is a vehicle for the faith, not the end of it.

Finally, I stay in the church because the sexist church I love needs women for its own salvation. The truth it holds, women test for authenticity.

We are sanctifying one another, this church and the women who refuse to be silent, refuse to be suppressed. What each of us sets out to convert will in the end convert us as well. Women will call the church to truth. The church will call women to faith. Together, God willing, we will persist, women despite the madness of authoritarianism, and the church regardless of the irritation of unrelenting challenge. We will perdure together. We will propel ourselves to the edges of our potentials for holiness.

"Why does a woman like you stay in the church?" a woman asked me from the depths of a dark audience years ago. "Because," I answered, "every time I thought about leaving, I found myself thinking of oysters." "Oysters?" she said. "What do oysters have to do with it?" "Well," I answered her in the darkness of the huge auditorium, "I realized that an oyster is an organism that defends itself by excreting a substance to protect itself against the sand of its spawning bed. The more sand in the oyster, the more chemical the oyster produces until finally, after layer upon layer of gel, the sand turns into a pearl. And the oyster itself becomes more valuable in the process. At that moment, I discovered the ministry of irritation."

I stay in the church with all my challenge and despite its resistance knowing that before this is over, both it and I will have become what we have the capacity to be—followers of the Christ who listened to women, taught them theology and raised them from the dead.

Forgiveness

The Bishop Who Said Sorry

In 1977, Joseph Bernardin, then Archbishop of Cincinnati, was president of the National Conference of Catholic Bishops in the United States. We went to a lot of meetings together, Bishop Bernardin and I.

One occasion was the twelfth Inter-American Conference of Bishops, a regular gathering. A few "observers" would attend, in this case, one male religious and three women—a Canadian, a Central American, and myself, then president of the Leadership Conference of Women Religious in the United States. The bishops, 26 of them, were not a large group, and so the "official observers" were unusually close to the center of the meeting. We all met together at the same table, ate together in the same dining room, prayed together at the beginning and end of every session, and sat in a tight circle in front of the altar for daily Mass together... until the day before the conference ended.

When I came into the large circular arena-like chapel that particular afternoon, no one was sitting in the Mass circle at all. "Joan," the other women stage-whispered to me from the pews that surrounded the altar area, "we're not allowed to sit in the circle any more. We have to sit back here," they motioned.

I felt the heat rise in my brain. Here I was in a church that never used a feminine pronoun in liturgical prayer, forbade altar girls and refused women the right to preach even when they had doctorates in theology.

What's more, women were supposed to bear their treatment as secondary members of the church with a docile smile, an unquestioning mind. But this was too much. Now they wanted us to be "observers" at the Mass, as well. So this is what I became.

I moved to the back pews and sat through the entrance procession with my arms folded and my hymn books closed. "Are you going to sit through the gospel?" the other women whispered. "There is no gospel being proclaimed in a situation like this," I said with my jaw set, and sat through the collect and the gospel and the communion, as well.

Joe Bernardin gave the homily on this Feast of Corpus Christi. His theme was the priesthood. He talked straight to the bishops but, judging by his furtive glances in our direction, was clearly aware of the women in the back pews. Immediately after the Mass, he headed straight for me.

"Joan," he said, "I told my secretary you wouldn't like the homily."

"Homily?" I spluttered. "What in the holy name of God does the homily have to do with it?"

He stopped. "You aren't upset because of the homily?" he asked, incredulous.

"Joe," I said, "I happen to think that women are called to be priests, too, but that doesn't mean that I don't respect and love the priesthood for its own sake."

"Then what are you mad about?" he demanded. "What is it? Come and have a drink with us before dinner."

"Never," I said. "If I can't be at the community table for the Mass, I have no intention whatsoever of going to any other table so that everybody can go on pretending that everything is all right for women in the church."

The conversation was a hard one. We had been put out of the

circle by the bishops, I said. "You were not," he said. "But I intend to find out just who it was who did it."

I was chagrined. "I'm sorry, Joe," I said. "I jumped to conclusions. We were told that the bishops didn't want us with them and I believed it. I apologize. It's not necessary to do anything. We'll just forget it."

"Oh, no, we won't," he said as he guided me down the hall to cocktails and dinner.

The next morning, before the opening of the final session, the bishops of North and South America made a public apology for the exclusion of women from the closing Mass of the week. A zealous sacristan, for whom Vatican II and women in the church were still at best a rumor, had made a judgment and been corrected for it.

I was impressed. But it wasn't over yet. That afternoon, we departed via the small airport in Medellin, Colombia. As we waited in a long line for the security checks, I realized that the women further up the queue had suddenly veered to the right. I stopped for a second.

Up ahead, two signs marked separate stations. The one to the left said, "*Hombres.*" The one to the right said, "*Damas.*"

Suddenly, I heard a call from the top of the line. "Joan! Jooooannn!"

There was Joseph Bernardin at the head of the row, head back, pointing up at the male-female placards and laughing. "Joan!" he shouted for all the bishops of the Americas to hear. "I just want you to know that I didn't have a thing to do with this!"

I laughed all the way to the plane, a little more wryly than he, perhaps.

Last year at Cambridge, when I heard about his death, memories of the laughter came through tears. Who is left who will apologize now?

Prayer

Monastic Prayer:
Unchanging Change

"Prayer is not asking," Mahatma Gandhi wrote. "It is a longing of the soul.... It is better in prayer to have a heart without words than words without a heart." In this particular area, though Gandhi's ideas are compelling ones, they are not new ones. The notion of wordless prayer and a hankering soul have been at the very core of monastic prayer life for centuries. As a result, though it is possible to talk about changes in monastic prayer forms, it is not possible to talk about change in monastic prayer life. There are some things which, even as they change, are changeless.

To the monastic mind, prayer is more than a fail-safe mechanism for souls faced with mystery and groveling for forgiveness. It is greater than a sense of spiritual obligation lost in a sea of ceremony. It is beyond a piety awash in fear of a dark and endless universe and in search of favors they cannot assure for themselves. A contemplative tradition regards genuine prayer more as an attitude of the mind in the face of mystery, clinging to hope and steeped in wonder, than simply as a gesture of contrition or obligation or supplication. The differences are not idle distinctions. One type of prayer is not the same as another.

What we think to be the purpose of prayer has as much to do with what we pray and the way we pray as the form we adopt in which to do it. In fact, what we think is the purpose of prayer determines the form we adopt. Therese of Avila, for instance, was targeted as an object of the Inquisition, not because she didn't believe in prayer but because the personal quality of her prayer life—her departure from formula and her level of personal conversation with God—constituted an excursion into the Protestant, according to those charged with guarding the purity of the faith from reformers and recalcitrants alike. God was a potentate to be approached with great protocol, not a personal presence to be cultivated. The form of the prayer was the form of the relationship.

Prayer is neither a passive nor an empty act. On the contrary. Prayer "works." The only problem is that when we pray we get what we seek. What we want out of prayer determines how we go about it. If we want security and protection, we say suffrage prayers; if we want serenity and enlightenment, we meditate; if we want immersion in the mind of Christ, we immerse ourselves in scripture. Prayer is not one kind of activity, it is many. It nourishes the spiritual life; it also reflects it.

When we are young religious, we "say" our prayers. When we get older in the religious life, we "go to prayer." But when we begin to see prayer as the undergirding of life, the pulse of the universe in the center of the soul, we become a prayer. First, as Gandhi says, we have words and no heart; finally, we grow into a heart without words. The truth is that the way we pray says something about what we believe about God and about what we believe about life itself. To the monastic mind, prayer is the marking of time and the pursuit of the known but unseen, the fulfilling but unaccomplished. Those qualities mark the prayer life of a monastic community in both form and substance.

Monasticism, a lifestyle built around the notion of community life and community prayer, changes slowly under any conditions. To bring an entire community to the point of change is not an executive act. It takes months, sometimes years, of preparation to form a community mind around a common concept. Interestingly enough, monastic communities change even more slowly than that where prayer is concerned. The years following the theological renewal of the church which had been inaugurated by Vatican Council II bear testimony to many changes, even in monasteries where time is measured more by the movement of a glacier than the movement of an arrow. But at the same time, some elements of the monastic life have hardly changed at all. Prayer is surely one of them. Consider it a sign of progress. Instead of changing one prayer formula for another, monastics rediscovered the purpose of the first formula and have recovered enough of its meaning and depth to renew them for centuries.

"A childish soul not inoculated with compulsory prayer," Alexander Cockburn wrote in *Corruptions of Empire*, "is a soul open to any religious infection." The thought may bear especially serious reflection in a busy world, even for monastic types. We can get so busy doing so many good things that we don't have time to pray. The soil dries up around our hearts and the tree of life within us dies. Then, a soul crying out for nourishment may be tempted to grasp at any nourishment that goes by, whether it really nourishes the soul or not. With that concern in mind, monastic rules require regularity, ritual and reflection as hallmarks of monastic prayer life. It is those concepts, not surprisingly, that have become the criteria of change. When those are satisfied, the prayer life of the monastic community is sound, whatever its form and schedule. When those elements are missing, the prayer life of a monastic community goes astray, the community becomes disoriented, meaning fades and what is meant to be a faith community becomes a collection of strangers doing work they could do with any other group of people in any other place at any other time.

Change has not been foreign to most monastic communities in the last twenty-five years. In fact, one of the signs of a vibrant monasticism has always been adaptation of prayer forms to meet contemporary needs. Benedict's last admonition after twelve chapters of instruction and organization of the daily *ordo* set the tone for the ages: "If anyone sees a better way, let them do it." (RB 18, 22)

Finding a better way to pray is every monastic community's single-minded purpose. It undergirds life. It energizes ministry. It gives substance to the contemplative life. With that in mind, adaptation has been a given; change, however, has not. Monastic prayer, whatever its form, remains forever communal, constantly rhythmic and steeped in ritual. The question is always what must be changed and what must not be changed in order to maintain these qualities at a pitch high enough to bring depth to the daily, one long lifetime after another.

At first glance, the changes common to monastic prayer in the last twenty-five years seem to be a smorgasbord of popular fads, spiritual styles or liturgical pop art. In reality, all of them—however inspired by the age and a renewed understanding of the ancient elements of prayer—are more than passing fascination with contemporary style. They represent elements that are essential to monastic spirituality itself but which had been lost over the years under the impact of the prevailing culture or the dictums of the church. Language, silence, brevity and personal reflection have all been reclaimed from the clutches of formalization, recitation and overload that characterized the accretions of the ages.

Latin, "the language of the church," distanced monastic communities, along with the church at large, from the richness that lay dormant but only barely visible in the Liturgy of the Hours. With the return of the vernacular to daily prayer, psalms, scripture readings and literature from the great thinkers of the church, both modern and ancient, became available to communities during prayer time rather than simply as objects of study. With the language of prayer itself no longer a barrier to understanding, prayer became an excursion into thought, into ideas, into statements of faith and moments of insight. Prayer became a period of spiritual development, not merely a time to say the mantras of the faith. Even more interesting, perhaps, is the fact that with the rendering of the Liturgy of the Hours into the language of a particular people, the practice of adding suffrage prayers in English to community prayer periods in Latin—three Hail Marys to St. Florian to protect the community from fire, three Hail Marys to St. Benedict for a happy death—ceased completely. The need to add "devotions" to prayer ended when prayer itself became a devotion.

Language, the use of real language rather than formal language for prayer, restored the Liturgy of the Hours to its place as the spiritual lifeline of the community. Universal language, the elimination of sexist terminology from prayer itself, inserted communities into the center of the human race, called to the community mind the needs and sufferings of all humanity rather than of only half of it, and spoke, at the same time, of a greater God than the inadequate male artifact that had been passing for an all-spiritual Creator for far too long. It made theology true to its best self.

Brevity, too, a by-product of the renewal that shortened some prayer periods and eliminated others, did more than quantity, ironically, to bring depth to community prayer where once profusion of prayers had become more the goal than reflection. With the elimination of the minor Hours, *prime, terce, sext* and *none*—all designed to have been a Christian response to the Roman changing of the guard in honor of the Emperor-god—morning praise and evening praise, the poles of the day, took their rightful place in the monastic horarium. Resurrection and creation took precedence in a life centered in the paschal mystery.

Community prayer, in the monastic tradition, is designed to inspire personal prayer and reflection, not to smother it with ceaseless recitations. Now there was time to immerse a community in the psalms they were praying, the readings they were hearing, the hymns they were singing. Now there was time to sink into the Liturgy of the Hours itself, to bring the day and all its works to the bar of scripture and to learn from the heart of the psalmody what it is that we are lacking in our own lives.

Personal reflection rather than community recitation became the purpose of prayer. By praying in the language of the culture, eliminating prayer periods that reflected the needs of earlier cultural situations, inserting segments of silence into the prayer periods themselves, communities that prayed became praying communities.

The changes that were adopted did not minimize prayer. On the contrary. The changes restored common prayer to its rightful place in the heart of the community and made it a springboard to the heart of the individual monastic.

In the end, then, little changed at all in the prayer life of monastic communities. Prayer is still said in common, several times a day, in psalmody as old as monasticism itself. But it is said thoughtfully, slowly, with enough room for silence to enable us to listen to the God who is listening to us. Maybe the most important element of prayer that has changed in the last twenty-five years lies not so much in its forms but in our attitudes toward it. We have stopped "getting prayer in" and started praying again. It is regular, ritualized and intent on making the monastic reflect on life, its meaning, its purpose, its joys and its sorrows. Otherwise, prayer is not prayer. It is only a formula, a kind of prayer wheel existence designed to impress God with our fidelity. But the function of prayer is not to coax God to save us from ourselves. The purpose of prayer is to prepare our own hearts for the inbreaking of God, for the putting on of the mind of Christ, for the burst of awareness, when it comes, that God is not somewhere else. God is here, now, in our own hearts. Prayer is simply time put aside to seek the God who has first sought us. Change is not necessary. Unless, of course, it is designed to make changelessness possible. As Gandhi reminds us, "It is better in prayer to have a heart without words than words without a heart."

Sanctity

Icons, Rebels, Stars and Saints:
Holiness in the Catholic Tradition

"Saintliness," Jean Anouilh wrote in *Becket*, "is also a temptation." The truth of the insight simmers in the center of the soul. Or perhaps it should. The gnawing inclination to affect sanctity by pious gestures, the possibility of being seduced by false forms of sanctity, the allure of plastic saints who parade across the stages of our lives wrapped in incense and holy clothing while the world stays steeped in pain, expose the horrors of the "temptation to saintliness."

The Catholic tradition gives clear warning, strong models of a sanctity far beyond either the ethereal or the ascetic presentation of the self. Christian sanctity requires conversion to the will of God, immersion in the spirit of Jesus and commitment to the human community. It calls us to wrestle with the self, to take on the searing audacity of Christ and to give ourselves for the sake of the world around us. Christian sanctity is not the living of the law, it is the living of the life of the Jesus who walked the roads of Galilee feeding, curing, healing, and contending everywhere that he had come to bring the Reign of God. Its model is the Jesus who answered John's "Are you the one who is to come?" with "Go and tell John what you hear and see: the blind receive their sight, the lame walk, the lepers are cleansed, the deaf hear, the dead are raised, and the poor have good news brought to them." (Mt. 11: 4-6) Clearly, the Christian does not go to heaven alone. When the holiness of some of us is built on the invisibility of the rest of us, good honest sin, artless self-centeredness, looks better than pseudo-saintliness.

Christian tradition makes the point painfully clear. We do not go to heaven by our own merit. We do not go to the heights of Christian spiritual development by preening our souls on ritual and holding ourselves above the fray of the human condition. On the contrary. The Christian saint is the one who has put on the mind of Christ and so put on the broken heart of the world. Such are the people whose sanctity challenges the lives of the rest of us.

The notion occurs that what we may be tempted to spend our lives doing in the name of sanctity may not be worth doing at all. We may set out to be exactly what the world does not need and what Jesus would disdain as the mark of "a whited sepulchre." That kind of sanctity is a snare of immense proportions for the sincere and the swindlers alike. For the sincere it poses the specter of a wasted life; for the swindler it threatens exposure. On the one hand, to seek sanctity in the wrong places is to risk an empty soul. To assume that regularity of devotions and rigor of discipline is the stuff of sanctity is to assume that we can make gods of ourselves for ourselves by ourselves. This is sanctity untested. On the other hand, to pretend sanctity for the wrong reasons is to guarantee a distorted soul. To posture in front of the human race, without substance, without benefit of tempering, without the currency of human significance as basis of exchange, is to twist the fibers of our lives into a tapestry of nothing. Sincere as it may be in its excesses, enticing as it may be in its public allure, false sanctity—sanctity steeped in the self—is not Christian. Sanctity must be for something beyond the satisfaction of the self, beyond a kind of protective piety or a bid for public approval.

When we set out to be holy in the Christian tradition then,

what exactly are we setting out to do and how shall we know it if we see it?

Styles of sanctity mark every period of Christian history, some of them startlingly simple, some of them verging on the neurotic. Christian sanctity has ranged from both total negation of life and total proclamation of the Word. Choosing one from the other is the central spiritual challenge of every age. It has both personal and public meaning. Whatever its particular form in any given culture, the real saint has always been considered as much public witness as private devotee. Those were saints who touched the lives of others in significant ways as well as concentrated on their own.

The Christian saint becomes the Face of God at the center point of life, reminding each of us that we are called to do more than exist and to be more than a breath lost in the night of time. What we take as the models of our own lives, then, not only changes us but turns our entire world around one degree at a time. Sanctity is not a private devotion. The summons to sanctity is an invitation to choose carefully the way we spend our souls, to choose for the gospel rather than for the sense of the perfect self, or the preservation of the perfect institution, or even for the security of a very banal salvation.

Christian sanctity is greater than the self, larger than private piety, more meaningful than religion for its own sake. It is no single state of life, no single work, no particular set of circumstances. It is as diverse as a Judean desert, a wedding feast in Cana, a temple in Jerusalem. The best of Christian tradition finds its saints in crowds as well as in hermitages, on mountain tops as well as in caves, at the resurrection as well as at the foot of the cross, in the noisy as well as the quiet, in women who defy the system to build a better world and in men who give their lives so that others may have life "and have it more abundantly."

What the world calls saints, what "saints" call sanctity, says something to the rest of us about what our own lives can be. All of them bring to consciousness the notion that there may be far more to life than we are seeing. There may be far more in life than what we have managed to acquire. There may be far more that life demands of us than we are willing to give. Christian sanctity is clearly more a communal than a private concept, more a social than a personal process. What I am, the rest of the world has the right to be. What I am becomes benchmark for the rest of society as well. I carry on my back the obligation to be what the world needs me to be and I look in hope for those who have carried that same obligation before me. The Christian life requires a commitment to the life of the Christ who consorted with sinners, cured lepers, raised women from the dead, contested with the officials and challenged the state. It is a life of prophetic presence and selfless service in a world whose soul has gone dry.

Saints, as a result, have always been a part of Christian history. They are those who, clear of soul and straight of eye, chart their lives by remembering its meaning. Saints mark the way for those who come after them. They are the pathfinders, the models, the stars in the darkness of every generation who enable us to remember the glory of humanity as well as the magnetism of divinity. They give us promise of possibility in the depths of despair and hope in the midst of the mundane. They bring new light to those parts of life grown dull from neglect. They remind us at our worst of what humanity can be at its best. They give us new insight into old truths, a new look at the God in our midst who goes among us so that "the blind may see and the deaf may hear and the poor may have proof of liberation."

Saints have been used and misused, undervalued and overlooked, misunderstood and overrated in every generation. Some have been called "saint" in one generation and ignored in the next. Some have been underestimated in one time and overemphasized in another. But most have simply been the memory of the human race for greatness of spirit. Most have been simple people who, when thrust into situations of public meaning responded out of deep personal spirituality. The Sufi tell of the disciple who asked the elder, "Is there anything I can do to make myself enlightened?" "As little as you can do to make the sun rise in the morning." "Then, of what use are the spiritual exercises you prescribe?" "To make sure you are not asleep when the sun begins to rise."

Christian devotion is nothing more than preparation for Christian sanctity. It cultivates the soul so that when the moment for holy presence finally becomes imperative, we will have been prepared to grasp and grip and seize it. Christian sanctity is a great deal more than Christian devotion. Christian sanctity requires that we become what we seek so that others, in their own moments of spiritual contest, can have the comfort of it, too.

For those who ask, then, Why have saints? the answer is, Why not have saints? Every generation needs heroes. It is not that saints are humans who have become divine. It is that saints are humans who have become fully human, fully the best that a human can be, fully attuned to life at its most meaningful. The saints are those around us in tiny neighborhoods and spacious offices who confront us daily with the great questions of life and bring to them the answer of themselves.

We search for the signs of the best in ourselves at all times and in all places. We measure ourselves by the measure of those who have wrestled with the same angels, lived in the same darkness, borne the same heat of the day and come to triumph, come to light, come to a new consciousness of the truth of life despite the pressures around them and the struggles within. We look for those around us who make life's great Jesus-story real and true. We watch for those who have touched Jesus and become new because of it so that we ourselves can find purpose in stretching to touch it.

The problem with defining saints is the problem of defining standards. Who is to say what "sanctity" really is? In fact, can anyone else but I begin to know what I have been through in life and with what honor, what depth, what nobility? Can anyone know whether I have survived it with more or less valor, with more or less faith? Can anyone know what I have borne to be my best self? And does anyone really do it without struggle? They are questions of phenomenal import. St. Therese of Lisieux, whose papers were sanitized by her community for public consumption, was made to look to the world like putty in the hands of God. In the last days of her life, however, she writes in her personal journal, "I am assailed by the worst temptations of atheism." Clearly, lack of struggle is not of the essence of sanctity. It is struggling that makes for sanctity.

For centuries the church has confronted the human community with role models of greatness. We call them saints when what we really often mean to say is "icon," "star," "hero"—ones so possessed by an internal vision of divine goodness that they give us a glimpse of the face of God in the center of the human. They give us a taste of the possibilities of greatness in ourselves.

But sadly, two things have happened to the modern notion of saint: first, saints have become official; second, saints have become bland.

In the fourteenth century, after hundreds of years of identification of saints by popular acclaim, the Vatican developed a process and criteria to determine if the persons venerated by a local population were worthy of general emulation. The canonization process, for the most part, had both substance and merit. The proliferation of local saints by the people who knew them or were impressed by the fruits of their spirituality or the value of their works was a grand and perceptive gesture. If nothing else, it has something to teach us about becoming aware of the character of those around us, those standing beside us today, bringing the white heat of the gospel to the ordinariness of the circumstances. Nevertheless, this redundancy of good served as much to blur the character of greatness as it did to preserve its image. "Saints" sprang up everywhere as every area, every region, every city, every village scrambled for relics and patrons.

At the same time, an officially constructed canonization process separated the people in need of models from the very personalities and forces that had given spirit to their lives in the here and now. In most cases, only those reputations that lasted far beyond the life of the person nominated for sainthood were seen as fit for examination by the Congregation for the Causes of Saints. By that time, of course, their spiritual fame had often waned, their social influence dimmed.

The canonization process looked for the heroic in the good, separated the merely pious from the powerfully holy, wanted miracles as well as the proof of a good life to qualify a person for canonization, concentrated on professional religious figures to the prejudice of lay people, and men to the detriment of women, the rich rather than the poor, concentrated on ecclesiastical docility as a sign of holiness and judged cases according to the insights of centuries sometimes far removed.

To this day, the process keeps popular hysteria from becoming the norm of holiness. It also runs the risk, however, of reducing holy passion to the level of prosaic piety. It hazards sanctifying the insipid. It chances turning goodness into cardboard. It disqualifies from consideration people who fall in the course of rising to new human heights. It cuts holiness from a common cloth: the theologically proper, the ecclesiastically docile, the morally safe. As a result, it eliminates from regard an entire body of people because of whom the very soul of the world has been stretched but who may not be synchronous with the current ideas of the church, who may not even be Catholic, who may not be without signs of flaw and struggle. It leads, imperceptibly but almost invariably, to a theology of disillusionment, the notion that only the perfect, the Christian, give us glimpses of the face of God—Moses and Abraham, the Samaritan woman and Peter, David and Samson to the contrary.

Clearly not everyone who points the way to God for us may themselves be perfect. There are figures gleaming in their holy causes who are awkward in their personal lives. They are sometimes in confusion, as we are. They are often in conflict with themselves, as we are. They are virtuous beyond telling in one dimension and weak to the point of sin in others. At the same time, they hold a fire in their hearts bright enough to light a way for many. They are impelled by the will of God for humankind and they will brook no less. They stand on gilded stilts above the rest of their generation, their comrades, their kind and become a sign for all generations. They are a proof of possibility from ages past and a symbol of hope for ages yet to come. They stand in mute conviction of the age in which they live and challenge us to do the same. Most of all, they are important to us now. "One does not help only one's own generation," the Hasidim teach. "Generation after generation, David pours enthusiasm into somber souls; generation after generation, Samson arms weak souls with the strength of heroes."

Sanctity in the Christian tradition requires far more than personal piety, then. It assumes a life so rooted in the will of God, so committed to others, and so large in the scope of its concerns that it raises questions in the hearts of the rest of us about the quality of our own souls, the depth of our own lives, the value of our own choices. The saint confronts us with the heart of Jesus and the mind of God. The saint takes our breath away. We see in them what we know that we ourselves should be and hang our heads, not in shame but in contemplation. The saint does not preach platitudes; the saint cries justice and gives service until justice comes.

Christian sanctity requires public commitment more than personal piety, as important as piety is for the cultivation of the Christian soul.

Christian sanctity goes beyond the incarnation to the crucifixion, beyond presence to the other to the point of being willing to suffer for the other.

Christian sanctity holds up for all to see the standards of the gospel in a world that prefers charity to justice.

Christian sanctity brings each of us to our knees before the questions of the soul, challenges each of us to measure ourselves against a canon higher than our own, shows each of us the way beyond ourselves to others, beyond goodness to the gospel, beyond private and parochial concerns to cosmic commitment.

The saint sees the world as God sees the world and responds wherever they are, however they must, so that the Jesus who lives in them may live through them.

It is a dark and dangerous journey and means more than a fidelity to dogma, more than the preservation of doctrine, more than the keeping of the law. It demands high valor and great faith.

110

It lives hidden sometimes as Charles de Foucauld did with the Arabs simply to build a private bridge between Islam and Christianity. It becomes hugely public sometimes as did Bartolomé de las Casas in his defense of the humanity of the American Indians. It goes where it may not go and does what it may not do as did Catherine of Siena in her involvement in church politics and her criticism of the pope. It lives a fiercely abandoned life sometimes as did Franz Jägerstätter who alone of all his village refused induction into Hitler's army and was executed because of it. But always, always, it lives more out of principle than it does out of piety. It goes above and beyond the normal norms to show again God's glory waiting in the normal. It lives the daily in a way that challenges us all. And it is in no way amenable to the official standards of the day. Francis of Assisi stretched the mind of the church about wealth. Teresa of Avila expanded the vision of the church about the nature of private spirituality. Harriet Tubman taught the church in her courageous deceit what it could be in the face of fear. Monsignor Hugh O'Flaherty, Vatican official in World War II Rome, proved in his protection of Jewish refugees that the church was still capable of sanctity in a world full of sin.

Some hear the call to the demands of dailiness. Some prefer instead to make dailiness the excuse for not listening to the demands it really makes, for choosing piety rather than sanctity. Indeed, "Saintliness is also a temptation." Indeed, saintliness can be its own sin, in which case we must learn to repent the private little nests we have made for ourselves in the name of the spiritual life. We must begin once again to walk the roads of Galilee with the One who brings us into ourselves to wrestle with the demons designed to keep us there, beyond ourselves to a world in need, and above ourselves to see the world as God sees the world. We must become what we all think we cannot be if we are ever to become what we are all called to be: "icons," "rebels," "stars" and "saints."

Work

Work: My Share of the Life of God

Once upon a time, the ancients tell us, a disciple said to the rabbi, "God took six days to create the world and it is not perfect. How is that possible?" "Could you have done better?" the rabbi asked. "Yes, I think I could have," the disciple said. "Then what are you waiting for?" the rabbi said. "Go ahead. Start working."

The story raises three questions about the nature and place of work in life that plague humankind yet: Is work a human punishment for sin or an opportunity to grow in the spiritual life? Is work something to be avoided or something to be embraced? Is work the opposite side of the spiritual life or the ground of the spiritual life?

They are important questions.

If work is meant to be a punishment, then managing to get out of it must be the ultimate sign of spiritual development and God's blessing.

If work is one of life's unfortunate burdens, then work is to be avoided so that life can be lived well and perpetual leisure is a state of life to be striven for.

If work is the enemy of the spiritual life, then people whose lives are full of children and business and the struggle to make ends meet are condemned to spiritual infancy or, at most, to the theology of good intentions: the notion that a person can be saved even if they are too busy to pray. But they can never come to real holiness that way.

The fact of the matter is, however, that most Americans, according to a survey of the Center for Ethics and Corporate Policy, believe that their work is very important to their spirituality and they want a great deal more guidance about the integration of work with their faith life than they say they are now getting from their churches and synagogues, Protestant, Catholic or Jewish.

And they have good reason to think that way.

Scripture is very clear about the place of work in human life. Human beings were put into the Garden, the Book of Genesis teaches us, "to till it and to keep it." Paradise was not a place for social parasites, in other words. Adam and Eve, it is clear, were expected to take care of what they had been given. The Garden of Eden was not an episode in irresponsibility. The Garden of Eden was a place for creativity and commitment, for accountability and constructive action, for maintaining the fruits and guarding the legacy of their lives for generations to come.

No doubt about it: It is sin that made what we were meant to do more difficult to do. What was meant to be easy we must now, thanks to sin, do "by the sweat of our brow." But sin is not the reason we are doing it. On the contrary. Sin disrupted the vision, true. We are often confused about what we should be doing in life. Sin muddied the way, yes. We are often conflicted about how to go about a good thing. Sin broke the relationships that make work personally satisfying and socially valuable, indeed. We too often fight among ourselves now for profit and lose a sense of the purpose of the work. But sin is not the reason we work.

Genesis is explicit: We work to complete the work of God in the world. Work, then, may be the most sanctifying thing we do.

The question is, What does that mean to us today in our time and here in our country and now in our homes?

Two poles compete for contemporary attention when people

talk about work: One pole is workaholism; the other pole, pseudo-contemplation.

The workaholic can use work as a substitute for other things in life. Work can be a way to avoid a carping husband or a dull and loveless wife. Work can save us from the noise of the children or the consciousness of the bills. Work can be a shield from having to do anything else in life. Work can be what guards us from having to make conversation or spend time at home or broaden our social skills. Work can simply satisfy the compulsion to make money, money and more money. And that kind of work is a deep psychic torture, a plexiglass between work and life, an external antidote to a sense of internal emptiness.

Or, workaholics can become their work. If it is valued, they are valuable. If it fails, their entire life has failed. Workaholics identify with what they do, and when what they do is over—when they get sick or retire or lose a job—they are over, too. Their sense of self is over. Their joy in life is over. Their very reason for existence is over. It is a sad distortion of the will of God for human work, a tragic end to an exciting possibility.

On the other hand, the thirst for pseudo-contemplation is just as sad. To assume that life is for lounging and then to blame that kind of injustice to others on the search for God is to make a mockery of the public life of Jesus. When we were young novices, in fact, the novice mistress was quite explicit. None of us were allowed to go to chapel between prayer times. The message was quite clear, even in a monastery: Sloth is not a Christian virtue. Holy leisure was not a license to live irresponsibly. Co-creation is a mandate writ deep in the human heart. Work itself is holy.

But why and how?

Western culture has not treated work kindly. We have a history of serfs who worked like slaves and sweatshops that robbed people of their human dignity and basic rights. We have lived in a capitalism that bred brutal competition and unequal distribution of goods as well as inventiveness and profit. We are watching the poor get poorer even while they are working. We see the rich get richer even when they don't. And we realize that the middle class must work harder every year just to stay where they were last year. What can possibly be good about all of that? That depends on the work we do and why we're doing it.

In the first place, work is what we do to continue what God wanted done. Work is meant to be co-creative. Keeping a home that is beautiful and ordered and spiritually nourishing and artistic is co-creative. Working in a machine shop that makes gears for tractors is co-creative. Working in an office that processes loan applications for people who are themselves trying to make life more humane is co-creative. Working on a science project, on the other hand, whose sole intent is to destroy life makes a mockery of creation. To say that science is blind, that science is objective, that science is neutral when what you make is napalm and the components of germ warfare and plutonium trigger-fingers is to raise ethical questions of overwhelming proportions.

God the creator goes on creating through us. Consequently, to have a gift that can nourish the community and to let it go to waste because "cooking is woman's work," or "the more you do, the more they want you to do" strikes at the very heart of human community and the process of creation itself. Work, then, is to be done for its own sake, because it is good, because it is needed, because we have the gift for it. Work is not simply a means to make money so that, eventually, we will not have to work at all. Work is what brings us closer to what the kingdom is meant to be. And if our work at making the world a better place fails, have we failed too? "If you expect to see the final results of your work," an Arab proverb teaches, "you have simply not asked a big enough question."

But work is not simply a gift to others. Work develops the worker, as well. Work is the one exercise in gift-giving that always comes back to the giver. The more I work at anything the better I get at it. And the better I get at something, the better I feel about myself. It is the fear of being good for nothing that destroys people. It is good work well done that gives us the right to say that we are valuable members of the human community.

Finally, work is an exercise in love. Leo Tolstoy, the Russian novelist, wrote once, "The sole purpose of life is to serve humanity." It is what I have cared for that I grow to care about. People who tell you they love you but never do a thing for you, people who say they value the family but never join the family in any project, people who say they are about the planet but never do a thing to make the planet a more human place to live, fail to see that life is a venture in human development and that work is its key.

Work makes time worthwhile. Time is all we have to make our lives bright-colored, warm, and rich. Time spent on an artificial high is time doomed to failure. Time spent amassing what I cannot possibly use is time wasted. Time spent in gray, dry aimlessness is a prison of the thickest walls. But good work that leaves the world softer and fuller and better than even before is the stuff of which human satisfaction and spiritual value are made. There will come a moment in life when we will have to ask ourselves what we spent our lives on and how life in general was better as a result of it. On that day we will know the sanctifying value of work.

Work has been badly warped, badly misused in our society. The globalization of industry is being used to bring people into a new kind of slavery. US corporations are leaving North American soil to manufacture computer parts in Mexico where they pay poor women $5.00 per day to make the boards which they will later sell for $500 at the expense of the working class in both countries.

Success has become more important than value. The drive for success at work, instead of success in life, continues to make people ill and to destroy marriages and to increase the level of personal dissatisfaction.

Efficiency has become a god that will accept the sacrifice of people for the sake of the production line and the profits it promises. We use what will do a thing faster, not necessarily what will do it better. We hire people for profit and retire them in mid-life, without pensions, when they have served their use to the company and then go out and hire the next generation of young and cheap and indefatigable laborers.

Indeed, the sanctity of work must be reclaimed if humanity is ever to be reclaimed in a world wounded and imperiled by sins against the co-creativeness of work. The disassociation that comes from being only one small point of the assembly line of modern life has dulled our consciences and blinded our eyes to our own part in a world where death is our greatest export. The days are gone when the family that tilled the field also planted and harvested it together. Now owners own and planters plant and sprayers spray and pickers pick and sellers sell and none of them take responsibility for the pesticides that reach our tables. Scientists calculate and designers design and welders weld and punchers punch and assemblers assemble and none of them take responsibility for a nuclear world.

The implications of a spirituality of work in a world such as this are clear, it seems: Work is my gift to the world. It is my social fruitfulness. It ties me to my neighbor and binds me to the future.

Work is the way I am saved from total self-centeredness. It gives me a reason to exist that is larger than myself. It makes me part of possibility. It gives me hope. The philosopher-poet wrote: "If I knew that the world would end tomorrow, I would plant an apple tree today."

Work gives me a place in salvation. It helps redeem the world from sin. It enables creation to go on creating. It brings us all one step closer to what the kingdom is meant to be.

Work is meant to build community. When we work for others, we give ourselves and we can give alms as well. We never work, in other words, for our own good alone.

Work leads to self-fulfillment. It uses the gifts and talents we know we have and it calls on gifts of which we are unaware.

Work is its own asceticism. When we face the work at hand, with all its difficulties and all its rigors and all its repetition and all its irritations and accept it, we do not need to traffic in symbolic penances. What today's work brings is what is really due from me to God. And if we do it well, we will have spiritual discipline aplenty. What's more, when this is not the job we want but we cannot get any other, when this is not the wage we need to make ends meet but they will not pay more, when we see younger workers and more automated machines and job slowdowns begin to encroach on the work we once thought would be our lifetime security, then virtues of faith and simplicity of life and humility come into play in ways too real to be reduced to empty rituals or religious gestures. Then work becomes the raw material of wisdom and holy abandonment.

Finally, work is the way we really live in solidarity with the poor of the world. Work is our commitment not to live off others, not to sponge, not to shirk, not to cheat. Giving less than a day's work for a day's pay, shunting work off onto underlings, assuming that personal days are automatically just additional vacation days, taking thirty-minute coffee breaks in the fifteen-minute schedule, doing one coat of paint where we promised to do two, are not what was meant to "till the Garden and keep it."

Work is our gift to the future. It is our sign that God goes on working in the world through us. It is the very stuff of divine ambition. And it will never be over. The philosopher wrote, "Do you want a test to know if your work in life is over? If you are still alive, it isn't." As the rabbi and the disciple both well knew, God needs us to complete God's work. Now.

Simplicity

Simplicity of Life

Gregorian chant is playing softly on the small CD player in my office. The house is quiet. The fireplace is lit. It is, at very least, a charming and bucolic scene. The question is, Is it in any way a study in simplicity of life? In fact, does anything really qualify as a demonstration of simplicity of life anymore? After all, fireplace and silence notwithstanding, I spent an hour on the phone this morning trying to arm wrestle into compliance the little three pound computer on which I am now writing this article. Then, on Friday of this week I will cross the Atlantic Ocean to do a lecture tour with the same kind of ease I used to feel in going from the back door of our priory across the parking lot to the tiny rural school in which I taught double grades. Is that simplicity of life or isn't it?

And I'm not the only one with the problem: The UPS man tells me that carrying packages is a pretty involved operation these days with computer programs and delivery routes that crisscross the globe. Opening a garage door is a technological process now. Telephone operators don't answer telephones anymore; machines do. Then they connect you to another machine—and this one with

119

a recorded message. No doubt about it: pencils are museum pieces; horses are for show; home is a movable feast and getting to work has become a two-hour commute.

Yet the subject of the simple life never goes away. Poets tout the virtue of simplicity. Philosophers plumb it. Writers wax sad and serious about its glory, its necessity, its loss, its value, its virtue, its utter sabotage in modern life. Simplicity, it seems, has escaped us. Simplicity, it appears, is gone forever from a global, technological, mobile and massified world. I suppose I should feel discouraged at even the thought of trying to deal with such an elusive subject. The fact of the matter is, however, that I'm not. If anything, I'm less sure than ever that what we have called simplicity has ever really been simplicity at all. Not in the spiritual sense of the word, not in the way the ancients used it, at least. G. C. Lichtenberg wrote, "The noble simplicity in the works of nature only too often originates in the noble shortsightedness of those who observe it." Simplicity doesn't really exist, in other words. We make it up. It's a sobering thought. We kid ourselves, Lichtenberg implies, and scientists now confirm, when we assume that simplicity is simply an arrangement of indivisible parts of anything. There is absolutely nothing in nature which, by that definition, is truly simple. A one-celled organism is made up of atoms and molecules beyond count and all in intricate relationship to one another. Everything created consorts with something else and depends on it and is held in being by a system that is infinitely sophisticated, interminably complex. The fact is that life is not simple. The fact is that we must learn to deal with our complexities with simplicity.

So, are we chasing a theological rainbow, a poet's fantasy, an adolescent's dream of life without burden, life without stress when we even dare to talk about simplicity of life? No, I don't think so. We may, however, be chasing a vacuum when what we really need is substance.

The hard truth may be that simplicity of life is not necessarily life without things and days without fringe at all. In fact, life without necessities—grueling, unfair and involuntary poverty—

is not simplicity at all. Life without its essentials is, in fact, social obscenity, a moral responsibility that is incumbent on society at large. No, simplicity may far more properly be life without clutter, life without compulsions, life without a need to control, life that is committed to contemplative vision, whatever its ebb, wherever its flow, than it is life without things. Simplicity of life may better these days be what the poet-president Sister Madeleva Wolff, CSC, called "the habitually relaxed grasp" than it is life without a collection of gadgets that we never really wanted or needed anyway.

Simplicity of life may simply be more the ability to handle with single-minded unity of soul what life brings than it is to refuse to accept anything except what we are willing to accept on our own terms, sparse and basic as these may be. When rigid vegetarians, for instance, put other people under a great deal of strain cooking for them, I can't help but wonder how really simple that is. When people keep their own offices immaculate by leaving their personal debris in lounges and foyers and public recreation rooms, the question persists: Is that simplicity of life? I see people who handle their own schedules very well because they simply refuse to have their personal priorities interrupted by anybody else's needs. Everybody else is forced to bend to suit them—and so everybody else's lives end up more and more intricate, involved, difficult as a result. So who is really practicing simplicity of life in these cases: The people with controlled menus, controlled physical environments, and controlled schedules or the people whose own lives are twisted and stretched to make that kind of simplicity possible? Simplicity, I am convinced, is far more than having life on our own terms whatever its effect on others.

Simplicity of life in a complex and complicated world is marked, I think, by four characteristics: A life is simple if it is honest, if it is unencumbered, if it is open to a consciousness not its own , if it is serene in the midst of a mindless momentum that verges on the chaotic.

Of all those things, however, honesty is surely its bedrock, its touchstone. We live a simple life when we do not pretend to be something we are not. The graduate of a two-year associate degree program whose simplicity is sincere, for instance, does not affect an Ivy League background. The woman who works in a middle-class office does not feel compelled to buy her worth by spending every available penny on boutique dresses. The financially secure do not live in a maze of conspicuous consumption, buying simply because they can buy, heaping layer upon layer of things over the innards of their unsatiated souls. The truly simple person, in other words, lives a life that is perfectly at ease with itself, that is not seduced by titles and pedigrees, by masks and patinas designed to protect us from the truth about ourselves, to remove us from our origins, to save us from the consequences of our humanity. They do not need to drip with jewelry or cosmetics or clothes to hide their looks or know their worth or feel the value of their own presence.

Truly simple people live with dignity whatever life brings to them. For them, then, only the truth about themselves, pure and unadulterated, really counts. In a society that thrives on image and advertising copy and status it is one thing to equate simplicity with things; it is another thing entirely to remember where you came from at all times, whatever the status you have now achieved—and never to cut the cord. Simplicity has something to do with being willing to have it known that you are from Bethlehem rather than from Beverly Hills.

At base, then, simplicity of life has a great deal more to do with authenticity than it does with things, or else it would be a virtue only for those who had things to forego. Then simplicity would have more to do with classism, with a kind of social play called "voluntary simplicity," than with an attitude of mind that lets us stand in the midst of our worlds naked and unafraid, sure of soul and unencumbered by the seductiveness of the unnecessary and the cosmetic. It would have more to do with accounting than with what the ancients called "purity of heart," that single-minded search for the essence of life rather than for a grasping after its frills, whatever shape those might take in our various worlds.

If one of the major aspects of simplicity in a highly cosmeticized world is honesty, however, the second characteristic must just as surely be detachment. It is one thing to know who we are. It is another thing to be indifferent even to that. Today I have money and a job and a title. On some surprising day, I will not have even that. When that day comes, all the simplicity I have affected will be tested to the core. On that day, I will discover the hard truth that simplicity of life is not frugality of life; it is life unencumbered, life free of the things we own so that they do not own us.

"We own only what cannot be lost in a shipwreck," the Arab proverb teaches. The image is a startling one only because it's true. Yet, no more difficult lesson is ever learned. In a consumer society that depends for its very economic base on the creation of false needs, the very thought of not wanting more than we have becomes an economic heresy. The truth is that if we don't buy, people don't work and so the process never ends. We create what we do not need in order to keep our basic needs at bay. There is very little new in new cars, for instance, but the placement and design of the old gadgets. Clothes don't change, styles do. Stoves and refrigerators, kitchen sinks and bathroom fixtures aren't different from year to year, they're simply painted other colors. It is a miserable cycle of ever-accelerating wants fed by layer after layer of arguments without substance.

But who can stand the thought of winding up behind the times? So, we "keep up," and we accumulate, and we die under the detritus of our own lives. Every person in the house owns a bike, just in case all the bikes might someday, maybe, ever be wanted at once. We keep five pair of scissors because one pair is new and the other four pair—all slightly different, none of them different at all—are still too good to throw away. We keep a dozen non-matching water glasses for a house of three people. "Just in case; just in case; just in case," we tell ourselves.

The cupboards fill up; the rooms fill up; the basement fills up; the attic fills up with things we never, ever—not even once a year—need, hardly use, or don't know what to do with now that we have them. Is that simplicity? Or is simplicity more the ability to get rid of what we're not using rather than hoarding what we will never touch again? It is so easy to fantasize life in a cabin splitting wood than it is to give away the old hammers we own when we buy new ones. And yet whole segments of our population lack even one of all the things we replace so casually. The Arabs have it right. Whatever we now own is simply temporary. We're not taking it anywhere so what is keeping us from being willing to get rid of it now except, perhaps, the fear that real simplicity is an excursion into trust too demanding of soul to bear?

To face society unfeigned and to walk through the world with hands and hearts unencumbered frees a person for the basics of life. Freedom is the real purpose, the real essence of simplicity. We have insulated ourselves against life to such an extent that we can go for years without living it. Riding around in fine cars everywhere makes it impossible for us to feel the grass that breaks between the cracks of old sidewalks. Musak and Surround-Sound and stereo systems vented from basement to bathroom make it impossible for us to ever appreciate silence. Television saves us from talking to the people we live with for years. Simplicity, on the other hand, is openness to the beauty of the present, whatever its shape, whatever its lack. Simplicity, clearly, leads to freedom of soul. When we cease to be consumed by the need for what we can do without, when we cultivate a sense of enoughness, when we learn to enjoy things for their own sakes, when we learn to be gentle even with what is lacking in ourselves, we find ourselves free to be where we are and to stop mourning where we are not. We find that simplicity is an antidote to depression. The desert monastics tell a story that soothes the soul and saves the sincere heart from legalized simplicity. "Abbot Mark," the tales tell, once said to Abbot Arsenius, "It is good, is it not, to have nothing in our cell that just gives us pleasure? For example, I once knew a brother who had a little wild flower that came up in his cell and he pulled it out by the roots." "Well," said Abbot Arsenius, "that is all right. But each person should act according to her own spiritual way. And if one were not able to get along without the flower, she should plant it again." Simplicity is not the arithmetic of the soul. Simplicity of life is not really about things at all. Simplicity is about being able to take them—and to leave them.

Finally, simplicity of life manifests itself in perfect serenity. The simple person pays close attention to the agitations that eat at the heart. It is our agitations that tell us where life has gone astray for us, has become unbearably complex and eternally confused. If we lack simplicity, if we fret at every delay, become miserable at every change of plans, become miffed at every imagined slight, become irritated at every lapse of deference, become despondent over every lack of gadget, then God has been replaced in us by a god of our own making. Then the simple life, the sanctity of the present moment, the contemplation of the divine in the mundane, the "purity of heart" that centers us on the eternal that is in the now, disappears into oblivion. Then simplicity of heart becomes counterfeit. Chop all the wood you want, give away all the clothes you own, romanticize the praises of the pioneer life but simplicity has flown you by. There is simply no simplicity in a heart full of agitation, in a soul too distracted by a plethora of projects and products to recognize the One who is among us yet, but invisible in chaos.

No doubt about it, simplicity and serenity carry overtones of the same chord. Both of them ring of an imperturbability that comes from being rooted in a world beyond ourselves where the God who is Everything waits for us to find life at the center beyond the clutter of the commonplace, beneath the chimera of the image, behind the things that pass for God.

Simplicity and serenity, simplicity and honesty, simplicity and openness, simplicity and acceptance are synonyms too long kept secret. But without them simplicity itself is subterfuge.

"Seek God and not where God lives," the desert monastics taught. The lesson is an important one. We cannot play at finding God; we cannot play at life. We must live both unceasingly, intensely, consciously. We must come to see the world around us with the eye of God and respond to it with a compassionate heart. We must be single-minded about the purpose of life, stripped of its non-essentials, set on eternity and sighted by a single eye. The fact is that quiet days, soft music and nice fires may nourish a simplicity within us but if we can't deal with the arm-wrestling match that is life—honestly, openly, freely and serenely—then simplicity of life has escaped us yet. Life as it is, not life as we contrive it and wrench it and want it and demand it, no matter how good we define our wants to be, is the raw material of simplicity. Indeed, "Seek God," the ancients taught, "and not where God lives." Not where we say God lives.

Empowerment

Empowerment and Spirituality

I approach the topic of empowerment and spirituality with a great deal of respect and a certain amount of trepidation. After all, we live in a culture that has seen the dark side of both. Spirituality, clearly, has often been used as an excuse to be humanly irresponsible. And power has too often, God knows, been made a poor substitute for empowerment.

The fact is that to be real, spirituality must empower, and power to be holy must be grounded in spirituality. The Talmud says, "Never pray in a room without windows." Never pray, in other words, without one eye on the world around you or your prayer may become more therapy than energy. And Camus wrote once, "The saints of our time are those who refuse to be either its executioners or its victims." Spirituality, then, is not for nothing. Spirituality is not for its own sake. But what is the spirituality of power and what, exactly, is the power of spirituality? How would we recognize them if we saw them? How do we know when they exist and when they do not? And what do they have to say about the use of authority in the church and the world today?

In the pursuit of these answers, I suggest two companions in the process of coming to understand spirituality and empowerment: Moses and the Samaritan woman. One, Moses, had enough power to tame; the other, the Samaritan woman, had insight that impelled. The world of our time and the church of our time I believe may well need both.

Moses knew clearly what power was all about. He had overcome the enemy, brought down plagues on the nation, drawn water from a rock and parted the very sea. Indeed, Moses was an inspiring figure, a charismatic figure, a powerful figure, who talked to God face-to-face. Moses could well have been a tyrant, an authoritarian, a dogmatist, a harsh and exacting lawgiver. But Moses clearly had a spirituality of power that forestalled that. Power was from God, Moses knew, to be used for the things of God. He had contemplated it in the burning bush. He had heard it on the mountaintop. He had felt it at the Sea of Reeds. And he had held it in his own hands with the prophets of Baal.

But the power was not his, and it was not for hoarding. And he knew it. Power, Moses knew, was only given to be given away— and give it away he did. Moses gave his power to the people themselves. Moses, scripture says, chose those who were capable and appointed them as heads over the people. Moses didn't have to be the last word on everything, the final word on the work of God, the only word on the will of God. Moses used his power, too, to plead for their forgiveness from an angry God. "Pardon the iniquity of this people as you have forgiven them ever since Egypt," Moses insisted in behalf of the weary, faithless band whose impunity tested the power of God. And finally, Moses knew that the power he had belonged to God alone. Over the plains at Rephidim while the army of Israel resisted the army of Amalek below, Aaron and Hur held up the tired arms of Moses while he prayed with the staff of God in hand that God would see them through the conflict that he was powerless to change. There was no authoritarianism here, no arrogance here, no domination here.

Indeed, in Moses the spirituality of power is a clear one. Power is not meant to keep a people down; power is meant to build a people up. Power is not meant to be punitive; power is meant to challenge. Power is not meant to be consumed by a few. It is meant to energize the people as a whole. Power is to be wielded, Moses taught Aaron, only by those who judge through the "breastplate of decision," through the eyes of Yahweh, through the very heart of God. The very purpose of power, the only proper use of power, in other words, is empowerment.

The model is surely one we badly need today. In our time, the psychiatrist Rollo May has identified five kinds of power, each of them an exercise for Christian contemplation and a challenge to Christianity itself. May tells us that every act of power is either exploitative, competitive, manipulative, integrative or nurturing. Exploitation, competition and manipulation, May teaches, are power used to destroy. Exploitative power is power over another. Competitive power is power used against another. Manipulative power is power used to control another—secretly. We use people, and defeat people and control people, in other words, until finally, by destroying them, we destroy ourselves, our worlds, our institutions, our very souls.

Power used to target the globe for extinction is certainly ruthless exploitative power. Power used to suppress the national churches in the name of church unity disunifies while it coerces. Power used against a Charles Curran who questioned with love and loyalty but in support of a Bishop LeFebre who rejected an entire council of the church has got to be a power gone arbitrary. Power used to rape the environment, to poison the water and pollute the air of this globe is power run amok. Power amassed to protect the church from eleven-year-old altar girls and the erotic feet of women and the use of feminine pronouns is power gone inane. Power used to suppress thinkers in a culture and an era more dominated by questions than by answers is a ruthless use of power that will do more in the end to harm us than the questions ever will.

We are living in a world where power is being misused, in a globe that is seething with the issues of women and hunger and poverty and mass migration and nuclear devastation. We are living in a world where both church and state are writing new laws about flags and liturgical dances and language and dress codes while the world is reeling under a massive burden of pain. An ancient proverb states: "To be properly wicked, you do not have to break the law. Just observe it to the letter."

And we wonder why so few are listening any more. And the deterioration is all around us. These kinds of power are crying for a spirituality that empowers, for a power that pleads, and a power that frees and a power that gentles and a power that cares for the people. Nurturing power and integrative power, May insists, are the only hope of our times. We need a government, we need a people, we need a church whose vast, massive, overwhelming reservoir of power is used to bring people to life and the world together.

The church that has spoken out against godless communism must, in the name of God, use its power to speak out clearly and strongly against an unholy capitalism that is devoted to stopping refugees at the borders of the wealthiest nation in the world—our own. We need a government, a people, a church, who use their power to build people up rather than to block them out.

The church that says that man is made in the image and likeness of God must soon, if the very power of God is to be credible in it, begin to see God in the image of woman, too.

The arms race and tokenism and propaganda and patriarchy and the concentration on disloyalty oaths masking as loyalty oaths and the male captivity of the sacraments must give way now to empowerment, to the use of power that works for others and the use of power that works with others. Or wasn't that what the Exodus was for? And wasn't that what Vatican II was all about? Did we misunderstand both the Covenant and the Beatitudes, both Moses' priesthood of the people and the early Christian community, both collegiality and the canonical obligation of the laity—at least according to the new code of canon law—to express our needs and cite our concerns?

And if that's so, what are we saying? Should Luther's questions not have been raised? Should the pope be continuing to free souls only for money? When Innocent III declared England under interdict for having accepted the Magna Carta and limiting the power of a king—a thing, he argued, that was against the natural law—should democracy, therefore, have been forever banned? Has the spirituality of power been reduced to nothing but the trappings of authority? Well, we need prophets now. Let there be no doubt about it. The spirituality of power is key in a modern culture to the existence of the planet, and it is key in the modern church, as well, to the glory of the gospel itself.

To those whose God is system, the criterion for fidelity in times of confusion is seldom only truth. To those who question when the innocent are victimized by an unholy use of power, bureaucrats too seldom preach truth and too often preach obedience. Yet it was a wrong kind of obedience that bred the Inquisition and the cruel crusades. Surely the church deserves a better brand of fidelity than that. And we must remember Moses questioned God.

In times of confusion to those whose God is system, the criterion for fidelity is too seldom an appeal to values held in common and too often an appeal to unity based on silence. But silence was exacted of Galileo, and without gain. In fact, silence was exacted of Galileo with great loss of power to the church. And we must remember Moses argued with God.

In times of confusion, to those whose God is system, the criterion for fidelity is seldom honest search and too often a limiting brand of orthodoxy. But it was the poorest type of orthodoxy that bred the wars of religion.

In times of confusion, those whose God is system say dissent is unacceptable and so make indifference a virtue. Consequently, to save the whole, we so often feed the system martyrs one at a time, whom we then reclaim centuries later and thereby salve our consciences: 100,000 women "witches," Joan of Arc, Mary Ward, Erasmus, Meister Eckhart, Pierre Teilhard de Chardin. And yet, it seems, we have no record that the papacy of the Borgia popes was ever officially condemned. Nor do we know of the dismissal of any hierarch anywhere who failed to say a word about the gassing of the Jews, or the selling of slaves, or the extermination of the Indians.

System is simply no substitute for the gospel. And power is no substitute for empowerment. Where are you, Moses? We need you now.

Nevertheless, a spirituality of power is not enough. We need also those who refuse to be not only executioners but also victims. It is not enough, in other words, to have leaders with a spirituality of empowerment. We need Christians with an empowering spirituality.

Once upon a time a traveler said to one of the disciples, "I have traveled a great distance to listen to the Holy One, but I find the words quite ordinary." And the disciple said, "Don't listen to the words; listen to the message." "And how does one do that?" the traveler asked. "Simple," the disciple said. "Just take hold of the Holy One's sentences and shake them well till all the words drop off. And what is left will set your heart on fire."

Unlike Moses, our second companion on the road to empowerment and spirituality is quite ordinary—as we are, you and I. She is a woman drawing water from a well in Samaria, a small province on the border of Jerusalem. She has obviously struggled through life, making hard decisions, and, as a woman, getting little affirmation from the system. She was full of questions, and full of frustration, but she was full, too, of an uncommon sense of the presence of God and her own obligation to respond to it. The scene is so ordinary, so simple. To really understand it, you have to shake the words off. You have to ask, "What's the real message here? What really happened in Samaria?" Then, finally, you have to ask, as you read the account of the Samaritan woman, "What's really happening to spirituality in the church today?"

In Samaria, it was a revolution going on. The Samaritans, remember, had once been part of the people of God. But they had been conquered by so many empires that they had been cut off for centuries from the country of Judea and from worship in Jerusalem. As a result, they had gradually developed their own interpretation of the books of Moses and their religion had become overlaid with many cultures and with many faiths.

To the Jews, the Samaritans were impostors. They were simply pagans who pretended to be true believers. The hatred between the two groups had hardened over the centuries. No pious Jew would have any contact whatsoever with Samaritans. Jews did not travel into Samaritan territory. Jews did not talk to Samaritans. Jews would not even touch an article that had been handled by a Samaritan—much like white South Africans treat black South Africans today; much like white Americans treated black Americans twenty years ago though both called themselves American and both called themselves Christian.

And the even stronger part of the message, of the account of the woman at the well, is the fact that, in those days, too, no good Jew would speak to a woman in public, not to any woman—not to his daughter, not to his mother, not to his wife. The rabbinic law was very clear on that.

And no good Jew even thought about talking theology with a woman. The Rabbi Eliezer had taught quite clearly, "Better that the Torah be burned than placed in the mouth of a woman." No woman had legal credibility. No woman was permitted to give legal testimony in a court of law. What in heaven's name then would a woman know about messiahs and politics and important things? There is no doubt—women and Samaritans were outcasts.

The problem of the church today is that Jesus simply did not share that animosity for either. Jesus was traveling through Samaritan territory. The gospel writer, John, says that Jesus "had to go through Samaria." But that's not true. There was another route then, just as there is now. It simply isn't that Jesus "had" to go. No, the real truth is that Jesus *had* to go. Jesus simply had to go to those people because they, too, were people attuned to life's great search; because God lived, too, in them; because they were listening and because they, too, were spiritual people, people of deep spirituality. And because no one, no one, has a monopoly on the spirit of God.

And there, at that well, in public, Jesus talked to a woman, a Samaritan woman. And Jesus asked for a drink out of a Samaritan bucket. And Jesus even offered to give her water of his own. And then Jesus had a discussion with this woman about some very deep theological things—about the nature of worship, and the nature of salvation and the nature of Jesus, himself. It is to this woman—*it is to this woman*—that Jesus first says in scripture, "I am the Messiah." It is to a woman far outside the boundaries of any system, far outside the spiritual imaginations of orthodoxy, far outside the seats of power, that Jesus gives the word and the promise and the mission. And this Samaritan, this woman, understood who he was. And she went to tell the others. And on her account, the scripture says, they all believed.

The Samaritan woman was an ordinary woman doing ordinary things who got an extraordinary insight into the fullness of life and was given an extraordinary task in a pagan world and they listened to her. She was a prophet, an unacceptable evangelist, a powerless figure, an apostle without portfolio. She wasn't a man—and she was to give the greatest testimony of all time. She wasn't a Jew—and she was to announce the messiah. She was neither politician nor priest and she was given the gift of understanding and living water and power and empowerment. And they listened to her.

Well, there's a revolution going on in today's church, too. Like the Samaritan woman, people, very ordinary people, are discovering the energy and the insight and the power that comes with the spiritual life. And as it happens when the Holy Spirit gets out of the chanceries of the world, quite ordinary people are being spiritually empowered to seize some gospel decisions of their own. They've come to some spiritual conclusions: that sexism is a sin, that peace is possible, that communism is not all bad, that capitalism is not all good, that authority has limits and that the Word of God lives, too, in them.

And they're proclaiming those things. And they're demanding those things and they're living those things in the name of the gospel of our Lord Jesus Christ. Why? Because Jesus has turned their very ordinary selves, too, and their very ordinary lives into an extraordinary awareness of the presence of God—in them as well as in the powers that be. They have discovered the spirituality that empowers and, like the Samaritan woman, they will not be silenced.

And what the church really needs is more of them to spread the faith instead of the law, to be a sign of hope and contradiction—rather than authority and legalism—in a world that is hungry and ignorant and spending more money and talent and time on the potential destruction of the world and the definition of heresies than on the development of innocent people and the challenge of hard love in a poor, oppressed, groaning, wailing world. With an inner spring welling up inside of them, these spiritually powerful people are the message that God has better plans for us. Because when spiritual empowerment and empowering spirituality explode in people, there is simply no holding back what they have come to see. They know with the philosopher, Ramana Maharshi, "As you are, so is the world."

They know that they have been sent to do the Beatitudes in a world where two-thirds of the people are deprived of the basics of life; they know that they have been sent to be the sign of the call to gospel commitment in a world that wants power and profit instead; they know that they have been sent to become the Christ figure in a world that says "You get them before they get you," and in a church that says that women are inadequate images of Christ. They know that they have been sent to turn the world around—one heart at a time.

Some people whose power is threatened by the powerless still ask, "What would a woman know, what would a nobody know, about messiahs, about politics, about nuclear war, about values, about church?" And the answer is the same now as then, the same here as at the well. The spiritually empowered know nothing but Jesus. Nothing but the gospel. Nothing but the power within that comes from an empowering spirituality that is not for our own sakes but for the sake of the other. Most of all, they know they have been sent. And they know that somewhere, someday, someone with a spirituality of power will recognize the power of spirituality and listen to them so that the entire world, the whole church, can be empowered. For the sake of the gospel. For the sake of the globe.

And how can we be so sure of all this? Why, simply because we have already seen Moses, the liberator, and the Samaritan woman. We have as model a Moses who was brave enough and faithful enough to trust uncertainty to lead to truth and who used his power to create something new, not to control it. And the Samaritan woman who took power that had not been given to her so that the powerless could have hope.

Justice

A Spirituality for the Long Haul

Winston Churchill wrote once: "I would rather fail in a cause which I know must someday triumph than triumph in a cause that I know must someday fail." In a church where the ideals are so clear and the implementation is so slow, it is a particularly important reflection.

The Zen Master taught us: "The seed never sees the flower." In a world where everything is changing and nothing ever seems to get resolved, in a church where revelation comes an inch at a time, the notion of slow growth is comforting.

The philosopher said: "If I knew that the world would end tomorrow, I would plant an apple tree today." In a world where whole classes of people are oppressed and authority justifies its decisions on the basis of authority alone or on a tradition that is more manufactured than revelatory, the idea of never allowing the destructiveness of the present to defeat our commitment to achieve the ideal is essential.

Vision, sacrifice and hope are the caretakers of the future. Without them tomorrow is impossible and today is straw.

At the same time, it is not always easy to hold on to a vision in the face not only of imperceptible growth but even despite intractable resistance. It is, in fact, often genuinely difficult. When, for instance, we see the poor getting poorer and the middle class eroding in a world where the number of millionaires increases every year, the vision tends to fade. It is difficult to keep speaking out in a world that blames the victim for the sin and smiles patronizingly at their spokespeople from behind barriers of gilded cocktail glasses. When altar girls are the bane of a church that says the gates of hell shall not prevail against it, it is difficult to keep seeing that church as the treasure house of the gospel. When women go on getting paid less, worked more, beaten, raped and sold while both women and men the world over take it for granted, it is difficult to believe that either church or state is capable of seeing or of caring. It is difficult to believe that all the great words in the encyclicals and constitutions are more than smoke screens to pretend one reality while we live in the other one with malicious joy. When brown men and black men are enslaved in sweatshops while their wives and children scavenge for garbage because the first world is not willing to pay wages that will provide enough food for Third World people, it is difficult to go on beating on a mountain of injustice that never moves. Then flashes of vision and spurts of sacrifice and moments of hope are not enough.

What is needed then is not short term effort. What is needed then is a spirituality for the long haul, a constant, unyielding commitment to keep on critiquing what is beyond critique. What is needed then is an internal energy for justice that comes unbidden and simply will not die, even in the face of defeat.

That kind of spirituality, I think, is based on four realities: It demands a memory of church that is above institution. It requires an enterprise worthy enough to merit the waste of a life. It depends on an unquenchable sense of gospel truth. It assumes an unremitting dedication to personal authenticity.

"If you expect to see the final results of your work," an Arab proverb teaches, "you have simply not asked a big enough question." To sustain a stay in a dry and barren desert, it is necessary to be about something great enough to be worth a lifetime of unrewarded effort. The great questions of life are questions that do not admit of cheap and easy answers. They are rooted in the bedrock of the culture and demand the emptying out of souls before they can really be answered. The woman's issue is an obvious one, for instance, but it is not an easy one. That women must soon be seen as equals in the church, adults in the world, artists and thinkers in society is clear. The amount of education and analysis and protest and courage that it will take, on the other hand, to reshape centuries of warped and distorted and heretical thought patterns that have been theologized and institutionalized in the name of God staggers the mind. No single capital campaign will do the trick. No one speech will change the climate. No single law will undo eons of damage. It will take a million lives heaped on top of one another in the rotundas of congress and on the marble stairways of the Vatican to burst the bonds of arrogance and superiority that make God male and males more favored by God. For women and men everywhere who realize that they are about the fulfillment of Genesis, no amount of time, no expenditure of life will be too much to ask for the lives of women and men yet to come.

We have, Genesis teaches us, been put into the Garden "to till it and to keep it." Co-creation is a human responsibility that carries with it grave implications. There are simply some divine cravings in life—the liberation of the poor, the equality of women, the humanity of the entire human race—that are worth striving for, living for, dying for, finished or unfinished, for as long as it takes to achieve them.

But if the nature of the vision itself sustains, if there are some things that simply cannot be foresworn whatever the difficulties associated with achieving them, there is a torrent even more demanding that propels a person on past resistance, despite resistance. The inexorable tide of the gospel message is simply too strong to resist. Teresa of Avila in *The Interior Castle* writes, "This is the reason for prayer, my daughters, the purpose of this spiritual marriage: the birth always of good works, of good works."

The person immersed in the spiritual life finds out all too soon that prayer is not a massage. Prayer is an opening of the self so that the Word of God can break in and make us new. We do not pray in order to change God. God is not a magic act we use to save us from the human condition. No, we pray so that God can change us. God is the One, the All, the Best in whose image we have all been made and to whom we must aspire, all lesser images to the contrary.

The problem is that once the change occurs, once the image of what we were meant to be seeps into our souls, once we see the Jesus who cured lepers despite the thinking of the institution that sickness was the result of sin, we can no longer stand quietly by in our own time while AIDS patients are ignored or worse. Once the way that Jesus treated women begins to puncture the hard wall around our hearts, no amount of "tradition" can blur or justify the aborted vision with which we live today. Once we see the Jesus who questioned Herod and challenged the Pharisees and contested with the High Priest, there is simply no way that we can stand by mute and satisfied while systems rest heavy on the backs of non-union laborers in Mexican *machiladores* or on scavengers in the Philippines or on welfare mothers in rat-infested apartments in New York slum hotels. Prayer unmasks. Prayer converts. Prayer impels. Prayer sustains the journey to justice from the first sound of the psalms to the last words of the Ascension. A spirituality without a prayer life is no spirituality at all and it will not last beyond the first defeat. For those who have tasted contemplation, the thirst for justice burns the heart out and will not be damped, whatever the wait, however dear the cost.

The eye of God and a soul of prayer are not enough, however, if we lose sight of the struggle that has brought us to the point on which we stand. An asceticism of the present demands a lover's heart. It is always easy to criticize the church and sometimes hard to transform it. At the same time, there will be no tomorrow for the church, if we forfeit its fragile present or fail to understand the beauty of the yesterdays that have brought us to this needy, but growing, place. It is after all the church that is the reservoir of the unfinished truth which fires us. It is the church that is keeper of the sacraments that nourish us. It is the image of those who bore the church on their backs before this age—Francis, Teresa of Avila, Martin Luther, Catherine of Siena, Ignatius, the women religious who persisted in their radically holy lives when it was the church itself who said they were not religious, and the men who spoke truth after truth and were silenced for it—who feed the hope that lies in us. Without those moments of revelation and grace, everything else is useless. But with them, anything is possible and the insanity of the long haul becomes the only kind of sanity worth having.

Finally, a spirituality for the long haul is based on a commitment to personal authenticity. If the vision has value and the prayer has depth, then a person cannot do otherwise than struggle and strive for the coming of the will of God, however slow its dawning. There is always the need to be true to oneself. When a person of prayer, a person of vision, begins to work in behalf of the poor, it is impossible to do otherwise. When a person of heart, a person of soul, begins to contest with the forces of patriarchy, it is impossible to do otherwise. When a person of hope and a person of faith start down the long path of prophetic action, it is impossible to turn aside to lesser things. That's why prophets are so dangerous: they cry in season and out of season, politely and impolitely, loud and long. And they do it because, having prayed the vision, they cannot live with themselves and do otherwise.

"It is not your obligation to complete your work but you are not at liberty to quit it," the Talmud teaches. The person who sees the world as God sees the world, whose prayer life is more converting than comforting, who walks in the footsteps of the those who loved the church to life in hard times past, whose sense of personal integrity is deeper than the need for social approval, is in for the long haul. They are willing to fail in things that must someday succeed; they are willing to be seed scattered and sown; they plant apple trees in wintertime.

Ministry

*Jesus at the Healing Pool of Bethsaida:
A Model of Contemporary Ministry*

There is absolutely nothing in scripture that leads us to believe that proclamation of the presence of Christ is a comfortable thing. Jeremiah ran through the street naked to get people's attention. If I read correctly, Esther was forced to face death for her people, because she went uninvited to a king who wanted no part of her message. If there is accuracy in the story at all, they ran Moses out of town.

It seems to me that scripture is proof that to give leadership in ministry, to proclaim the Redeemer in our time, will have nothing whatsoever to do with getting promoted or fitting in or being establishment or being approved. In fact, it may be—I think scripture implies it—precisely when we find ourselves at the top of an institutional pedestal, at the top of any institutional pedestal, that we are in the least danger of proclaiming the presence of the caring Christ.

The question then is, How can you and I possibly know what it means to walk in justice or to proclaim a Redeemer, to make an option for the poor, to seek peace? The answer, I believe, is at the healing pool of Bethsaida. I think that Bethsaida is really the place where a minister in the church today needs to go to discover what proclamation means, what empowerment does.

Why? Because the healing pool at Bethsaida is an object lesson in faith, in obedience and in empowerment. Remember it with me for just a moment, the Gospel of John 5: 1-12. Think about it. Think first about Bethsaida. Bethsaida was one of those places and moments in life that was on the very edge of life. Bethsaida was a breakthrough, breakdown world. Great things happened at Bethsaida, great things.

The problem was that tragic things happened at Bethsaida, too, and all for the same reason. Bethsaida is a place in scripture that is alive with possibilities. Bethsaida reeks with power. And Bethsaida is a tragic center of the oppressiveness of possibilities never fulfilled.

Breakthroughs did happen at Bethsaida. Everything was not bad there. The scripture reads, "Every year the waters stirred, and those who got there first were healed." For everybody else who comes to Bethsaida, Bethsaida breaks down hope. Bethsaida breaks down promise. Bethsaida breaks down proclamation. Until one day when Jesus comes.

Jesus comes walking very purposefully. He walks through this rushing, running, pushing, shoving, expectant crowd. He walks among the blind and over the lame and around the paralyzed, and not to the water. Jesus goes straight up the hill to the very farthest edge of the crowd and stands, himself upright, in front of one who has not walked upright his whole adult life. Jesus goes straight to the one who has been overlooked and pushed down and pushed out of the stream of life at Bethsaida year after year after year.

"Don't you want to be healed?" Jesus asks. The forgotten man answered, "Sir, there is no one to carry me down."

What's to be proclaimed here? What does power imply here? After all, the paralytic had his chance. That's the way life is. You have to get very, very real about these things. You can't just go off into flights of fancy. The fact of the matter is that some people just do not have the nerve. Some people do not have the character.

Some people do not have the gumption.

So the system is set: there are rules, policies, circumstances. The situation is clear: if you work hard, you get ahead. To violate the Sabbath, to tamper with the cultural expectations would only do more harm than good, Jesus. What would the bishop say? What will the benefactors do? After all, it has been thirty-eight years. What harm will it do to wait a little longer? Do the right thing, Jesus. Tell him to come back tomorrow when the office is open. Surely that can't be asking too much.

What is the point? The point is that what happens at Bethsaida does not depend on the paralytic. What happens at Bethsaida depends on the faith and the leadership of the one who chooses to be minister. It is what the proclaimer, the leader, the minister, believes that faith demands in a situation like this that will make Bethsaida either a breakthrough or a breakdown place for everyone.

The history of spirituality is very clear about identifying three possible faith responses, proclamations, to any paralytic at any healing pool named Bethsaida.

The first type of faith proclamation is the intellectualist approach. The intellectualist in history is always concerned about knowing God and mystical illuminations and contemplation. The problem is that too often intellectualism taken to an extreme winds up being a lack of commitment to the earthly city. The intellectualist at Bethsaida is the one who says to the paralytic, "Now this situation will make you very close to God. All you have to do is offer it up, because God wills it for you."

God wills some of us black, some of us Hispanic, some of us women, some of us poor. The intellectualist nicely dichotomizes religion and life and history and heaven. For the intellectualist, the church is primarily and most of all a set of doctrines, a range of beliefs, a type of institution to be proclaimed and led and ministered to. The intellectualist always talks a lot about faith, and says, "Our function is to wait for union with God."

Then there is the relational or personalist proclamation. The personalist believes that leadership in ministry in this situation must always look to the personal beneficence of God. The relationalist or the personalist is a very devotional person. The personalist at Bethsaida says a rosary, finishes the novena, recalls that cursillista mantra, and sits down with the paralytic to wait for the waters to stir next year. The personalist talks a lot about building community. They talk a lot about love.

A third response that can be brought to Bethsaida in the history of spirituality is performative. Performative leadership in ministry says that you cannot have a full proclamation of the gospel unless the Word becomes transforming action. In other words, performative leadership in ministry is a commitment to the upbuilding of the kingdom by establishing on earth a just society that reflects the coming of the reign of God in our lives.

Leaders with performative faith who set out to be ministers in the church at Bethsaida are "Our Father" people. They pray every single day, "your kingdom come, your will be done." Then they do something. For a person whose faith and ministry is performative, the church is a servant. The servant church goes to Bethsaida, not simply to appear, not simply to preach there, not simply to be a warm presence there. A servant church always goes to Bethsaida to see who needs to be carried down.

What is the problem? As I see it, the problem is what it has always been—the entire world is back at the healing pool at Bethsaida. While they look for leadership, look for ministry, look for justice, look for Christianity, the Bethsaida of our day is still a whirling, bubbling, promising, and oppressed place.

Half the population of the world is disenfranchised: women and children who have little or no part in the decisions of government or economics or social stratifications that affect them. Air and water pollution are poisoning our people. We have lost one-fourth of the Amazon jungle and with it one-fourth of the oxygen it supplied, to copper mines that never replanted the land. The American Cancer Society says that 80% of the cancers in this country are due to environmental causes, technological dangers and toxic wastes.

In the early 1980s, UNESCO administered a test to social

studies teachers throughout the world in one hundred countries. The US teachers ranked 100th out of one hundred in that test. The name of that is "global illiteracy" by a country that wields more effect on global issues than any other.

When I was a teacher in grade school, we used to teach that the major export of the United States was wheat. Now the basis of our import-export system is weapons. We will sell to anyone who will pay. We have sold weapons to our friends to fight our friends. We have sold weapons to our enemies to fight our friends. We have armed enemies to fight enemies. We have armed friends who became enemies.

We are a country, according to the November 1983 issue of *The Monthly Review*, that has threatened the use of a nuclear weapon nine times since World War II, six times against non-nuclear countries, and always for political rather than military reasons. We weren't threatened, we simply didn't like their internal politics. It was not because anybody had crossed our borders or threatened any of our ground. How can we possibly say that we are interested in leadership in ministry, that we are interested in the upbuilding of the church, and not see these as basic creation issues?

Let me put it this way. Assume the world is a village of 100 people. Six of those people consume two-thirds of its goods while the other 94 sit on their front lawns and watch them do it. No wonder those six buy so many guns.

If you and I are going to give leadership in ministry, we have to come to grips with that village and realize that it is a very familiar place. In the *New York Times*, June 1987, a poll of American college freshmen indicated that year's American college freshmen were much less interested in pollution and racism and philanthropy and a philosophy of life than any class before them for the last twenty-five years, and much more approving of cohabitation, financial security, and abortion. Those are the people we are putting into the mainstream of the church.

Indeed, Bethsaida is happening all around us. The waters stir today, too. They stir for the wealthy, for the West, for white males.

It's not true that the whole system is in chaos. Some people are getting on, getting up, getting rich. But others wait their turn and are denied.

Who will see the situation? Who will be healed of their own racism, sexism, militarism, parochialism, nationalism? Who will hold themselves accountable for the oppression of others and learn from scripture that somewhere along the line you must begin to do away with the process and politics of it all? Who will take up the option for the poor and proclaim the redeemer to them as Jesus did? Not by saying, "Offer it up." Not by saying, "Let me hold you up." But by cutting right through the system and saying, "Get up," and then by staying there to help raise them up.

Do you want a test of the reality and depth of the leadership in your own ministry? Ask a friend to tell you three things for which you stand and three things you did to prove that. Do you stand for the just distribution of resources? Do you really stand for peace and nuclear disarmament? Do you really stand for the equality of women in the church and society? What did you do that would prove that?

I am not saying that everyone is guilty. I am saying that everyone is responsible. I am saying that the questions are important because this time it is our turn at Bethsaida. What we proclaim and how we proclaim it may well make the difference in a world that hasn't stood up straight in at least 38 years.

Two key pieces of research give real insight into what it means to proclaim the redeemer in a system, to a system that wants profit, not prophecy. In the environment spawned by World War II, Gertrude Stein said, "The most important thing for Germans to learn is disobedience." In 1973 American sociologist Gerda Lederer studied authoritarianism which she defines as a willingness to submit uncritically to authority, a disposition to blind obedience. She further identified authoritarianism as a hallmark of German culture, visible in German institutions from Bismarck's army to the Hitler Youth Movement. This predisposition has been used to explain the fact that German Christians complied with the Holocaust. Hitler is not entirely to blame. The fundamental problem was that the German people permitted massive evil, in resistance to evil, out of blind obedience. But, by 1973, German youths were less authoritarian than were Americans. Worse, the Milgram studies at City University of New York from 1966 to 1974 showed that two-thirds of the study participants were willing to inflict severe pain on other persons simply because they were directed by an authority figure to do so. They never questioned the reasons for or the results of their actions—they followed orders on the assumption that if the authority figure said the action was necessary, it must be. In the same period, D. C. Bok established a correlation between religious belief and obedience to destructive commands. Religious believers were consistently more obedient and more willing to inflict more pain than any other group.

Lawrence Kohlberg has described six stages in the development of moral maturity:

At the lowest level of moral development, we obey out of a punishment/obedience orientation. We bow to a superior power to avoid punishment. These are the people who do good in the church to avoid hell.

The level above this is called personal interest. I obey in order to gain satisfaction for my personal needs. The motive is to obtain a reward. It is a vending machine mentality: If I do my part, then God does God's part and we all come out even.

The third level is the good child orientation. We obey to gain approval and acceptance.

At the fourth level, Kohlberg says, we do good in order to maintain the laws and to keep order. Our loyalty is to the system. To maintain the system is characteristic of this level. The motive here is to avoid guilt. These people are into perfectionism, legalism and following orders, "Whatever the boss says."

Those at the fifth level obey because of what they believe is good for society in general. "I am doing this not because I am resisting my community but because I love my community."

The highest level of moral maturity is conscience orientation, obedience to conscience grounded in abstract, ethical principles: justice, equality and dignity of life. Here, the motive is to avoid self-condemnation. Here are Plato, Christ, Thomas More, Martin Luther King, Jr., Dorothy Day.

Kohlberg adds four other things about moral maturity: 1. Moral maturity is progressive; no steps can be skipped. 2. The development can be stopped. 3. It never regresses except perhaps under the impact of mental illness. 4. It requires role models for development. I cannot get to the next stage unless I see someone who has been there, unless it is modeled for me.

The point is that to proclaim the redeemer in our time, to bring leadership to the church in our time, to be a prophetic conscience in the church presumes more from you and me than simply preaching or personality. It will require a prophetic presence. This generation is watching us for leadership in a world where science and not industry has become the great high priest of our time. The motto of industry, "The greatest number of desirable goods for the maximum number of people at the cheapest possible cost," is dead. The motto of science, the new motto of our society is, "What can be done must be done and it will be done whether it ought to be done or not." It is not the limits of the marketplace but only the limits of the mind that are determining the products that are controlling us.

We live in a world where technology has not made the world smaller but where technology has made the world one. War in the Middle East interferes with the production of oil and stops transportation in the West. Scenes of famine in Africa are shown on television in American restaurants; scenes of American three-car garages are shown on street corner television in Third World villages.

Decisions which make a corporation wealthy in one country make everyone poor in another country. Who will take leadership and minister to American economic policy? Or has religion once again become a localized, tribalized collection of national gods, and the American god is a good god?

We are ministering in a world where Christians have invented the high art of planetary cataclysm. Christians argue matchstick parity at every rectory cocktail party in the country. Matchstick parity—that's when we sit around discussing the nuclear era and talking, in a situation where we are up to our neck in gasoline, about who has the most matches when it will only take one of them to do the job. We live in a world where the end of the world has been created and it is stored in the cornfields of Kansas. Who will prophetically proclaim the presence of the caring Christ to American foreign policy? Proclamation is not preaching; proclamation now requires that we live prophetic lives in a world where prophets are few and the people are poor.

If you are in a ministry in which you choose to be a prophet, remember that scripture describes four kinds of prophets:

The prophets of Baal claimed to minister by being great cultists. They prayed and whirled and liturgized and dogmatized. But never—not once—were they able to make life better for anyone. They were simply the window dressing on the religion. Their leadership was no leadership at all to the poor, the displaced, the defeated, the destroyed.

The prophets of the court claimed to be ministers too, but they told the king exactly what the king wanted to hear: "You are the greatest king; you are righteous. You will win because you are most blessed and approved by God." The prophets of the court said exactly what their kings wanted them to say, and they led a lot of kings to death. What kind of proclamation of ministry, what leadership was that for the country, for the kingdom, for the young men condemned to die in old men's wars for conscienceless kings?

The third type are the sons of the prophets. Scripture is very gentle with the sons of prophets. They were very good people who obeyed the authorities, lived the laws, kept the fasts and guarded themselves against the world so that they would not succumb to it. What kind of proclamation of a loving God was that to the confused, the exploited, the sincere, the struggling?

Only the prophets of Yahweh, who accepted responsibility for insights they did not seek, to speak out to people who did not want to hear about the continuation of the covenant of justice with Yahweh, preserved Israel and kept it effective in the world.

Only through those prophets, the true prophets of Yahweh, did the oppressed and denied and outcast hear and see and feel the proclamation of the redeemer. Only by them was Israel given hope.

And that's how Jesus came to Bethsaida: as a proclaimer of hope to the paralyzed, overlooked, unattended other in the face of a rigid system that was not all bad but definitely unjust. Therefore that task is also ours. Like Jesus and the prophets, conscience commits us to make a pleasing sacrifice, to walk in justice, to proclaim the redeemer to our time.

When the paralytic went to Bethsaida, he didn't go in faith. He didn't need faith, he knew the waters could heal. He had seen it happen year after year. When the paralytic went to Bethsaida, he didn't go for love. He already knew the presence and power of a loving God. No, when the paralytic went to Bethsaida, he went in hope, looking for a real proclamation of redemption, looking for someone to carry him down.

We do not have a crisis of Christianity. No, we have a crisis of significance, a crisis of spirituality which leads us to a crisis of contemporary credibility, of institutional structure called "church," and of the prophetic proclamation of hope.

Augustine says that, of the three theological virtues of faith, hope and love, hope is greatest. He writes, "Faith only tells us that God is real and love only tells us that God is love. But hope tells us that God will work God's will. Hope has two lovely daughters, anger and courage: anger so that what must not be, cannot be. Courage so that what must be, will be."

My prayer is that in our Bethsaida, where again the waters stir for some but not for all, that in our proclamation of the redeemer, there is a touch of anger, a burst of courage.

Stewardship

*Monasticism: An Ancient Answer
to Modern Problems*

We have, as a people, tried every new trick we know to balance our desire for "the good life" with its effects. We've increased our technology, multiplied our laws and expanded our educational efforts, but nothing seems to be working. Maybe it's time to try anew what worked well enough to save a civilization centuries before us so that it might save us again.

The fact is that for one set of values—hard work, respect for the land, simplicity, care and stewardship—our generation has preferred another criteria: profit, consumption, quick returns, short-term gains and instantaneous gratification. The result, it seems, is a society that is destroying itself at the hands of its own success.

Crops have never grown either so fast or so big in the history of humankind and yet more people every year starve to death on barren land. Water has never been so conductible and yet so unusable. Paper has never been so in demand in all of recorded civilization and yet the cost of it has never been so high. Travel and the interaction between peoples have never been so common and yet national security has never been so slim. People have never been employed in larger numbers by major industries in every country of the globe and yet whole masses of people have never been poorer or less able to sustain themselves.

What we call the "underdeveloped" countries of the world have been supplying natural resources and human labor for the needs and wants of the West for generations now, but never getting richer themselves and never, obviously, getting developed.

The question, of course, is, Why? And the answer is crucial to all of us because this time it is the globe and not the neighborhood or the nation that is at stake.

The Sufi tell a story that may best illustrate the problem and a very ancient, very modern spirituality gives us a model that may best demonstrate its answer. The Sufi tell the story of a people who were searching for fullness of life: "There are three stages in one's spAniritual development," said the Master, "the carnal, the spiritual and the divine." "Well, Master," the eager disciples asked, "What is the carnal stage?" "That's the stage when trees are seen as trees and mountains as mountains," the Master answered. "And the spiritual?" the disciples continued. "The spiritual is when one looks more deeply into things. Then trees are no longer trees and mountains no longer mountains." "And the divine?" the disciples asked in awe. "Ah, yes, the divine," the Master smiled. "Well, divine enlightenment," the master said and chuckled, "is when trees become trees again and mountains, mountains."

We have a great deal, it seems, to learn from the story ourselves. Even a superficial analysis of the last fifty years, let alone a study of the last two hundred years of shift from an agricultural to an industrial society, is clear proof of a continuing reversal in attitude about the concept of nature and our place in it.

In 1940 if a family bought a living room suite, they expected to own it for life, to move it into their first home, to raise their children on it, to have it be the centerpiece of the house when they were grandparents. People saw trees as trees in those days. If you used one, you planted one. If you shaped one to your own life needs, you honored the life in it and cared for it well and you kept it forever.

Today, living room suites and the trees that go to produce them are thrown away on a regular basis. One tree after another goes down to make new living suites for people who have grown tired of the ones before them. Today, trees are not seen as trees. Today trees and water and air and land have taken on the image of profit for the few, the image of affluence for the others, the image of need for far too many and, tragically, we consider ourselves "advanced" because of it.

In Mexico City, they need clean air but industries consume it with toxic belch at speeds far beyond the power of nature to cleanse itself for another generation and so the risk of brain damage hangs in every cloud of smog that droops between the mountains.

In Haiti, hillsides are stripped of trees for firewood because the poor have no other source of energy but, because of this practice, the valleys flood out every spring, destroying houses and crops and the lives of other people too poor to lose another thing.

In the Philippines, land of 1,000 islands, the water runs dirty and dangerous from open cesspools and unregulated industrial waste.

Worse, perhaps, than the fact that people are in a great state of natural deprivation and that the planet faces an eroding reservoir of resources is the fact that we have called all the human degradation that went along with such conscienceless profitmaking a sign of God's judgment on the lazy and the feckless and the spiritually immature. God blessed with material good those who were spiritually righteous, the theologians of the industrial revolution claimed. From this point of view, those who lack things lack them primarily because they lack virtue. Goodness, in other words, gives us a claim on God's blessing and prosperity is a sign of God's favor. All others, the evangelists of capitalism claimed, were full of sin or God would have filled their lack. As a result, we have come to blame the poor for their condition and to see it as no obligation of our own.

And there is lack aplenty. The problem is that it is not the morals of the destitute that must now come under scrutiny. According to the 1987 report of the UN World Commission on

Environment and Development, at least sixty million people died of diarrheal diseases caused by unsafe drinking water and malnutrition between 1984 and 1987 alone. And most of them were children.

Loss of life from environmental mismanagement and the droughts and floods that have resulted from it has increased by the millions since the 1960s, thirty-five million of them in the drought-stricken Africa of the 1980s alone.

In 1980, the report documents, there were 340 million people in eighty-seven developing countries so undernourished that serious underdevelopment and health problems were an inevitable prospect.

Indeed there is something immoral about all of that but this time it is the policies and stratagems and expenditures of the affluent nations of the world that must be evaluated. If the world that spends millions of dollars every day on instruments of destruction needs security and defense, it is surely food security, air security and water security that must have priority. Otherwise, generations to come carrying the responsibility to assure the security of their people but afflicted by malnutrition, may not be sane enough or rational enough or intelligent enough to do so without harm to others.

It is defense against erosion and defense against energy loss and defense against the ravishment of global resources that are key to national sovereignty and world peace. Like the Sufi disciple we have begun to see other things in the trees and mountains— profit, the good life, consumer goods, production—that we call Divine but which clearly fall far short of fullness of life for everyone. There must be more to the good life than this, we know.

The problem is, Where shall we go to find a model of what it takes to live globally if our own educational system and technological society and legislative policies are not able, apparently, to provide the standards that take us beyond a thirst for things, things and more things? More than that, What will have to change in our own lives if life is to continue to be lived at a level of decency and beauty and health and possibility and the globe is to be preserved?

The answer, I think, is two-fold. First, we must begin to re-examine our theologies of creation. Then we must return to the ideals that saved Europe once and were then abandoned for short-term gain. The answer, I think, lies in the history and values of a way of life devised in the fifth century and dynamic to this day.

Benedictine monasticism was a good gift for bad times. And the fifth century was definitely bad times for Europe. With the breakdown of the Roman Empire, the countryside was in disarray. Roads to market were prowled by thieves, the towns were unguarded and unserviced, vast properties were overrun, peasants were dispossessed, life was unsafe, unpredictable and undeveloped.

People sat and starved on untilled land or roamed and starved on unkept roadways as they searched for work and food from abandoned town to abandoned town where order was a thing of the past and markets had been long closed. The world of sophisticated cities that had been part of the legacy of Roman roads and Roman law and Roman guards and Roman administration was, for all practical purposes, over. Society had become a parade of rural villages where poor and uneducated people eked out a subsistence existence on dry and hardened land.

It was monasticism that became the economic fly-wheel of the age, the institution that provided a counterweight to chaos.

Benedictine monasticism was designed to be communal, stable and self-supporting. Unlike other religious figures of the period, monastics did not live solitary lives in desert cells or in woodland hermitages. They did not wander through the countryside begging for alms and food. They were not spiritual athletes whose piety rested on grand feats of fasting and human deprivation.

Benedictine monastics were formed to live a community life centered on God, in peace with all of humankind both within and outside of their own monasteries, and in harmony with nature. "When they live by the labor of their hands," the Rule of Benedict wrote, "as our ancestors and the apostles did, then are they truly monastics." (RB 48:8)

Most important of all, perhaps, was the fact that the monastics themselves were tied to the land. Where their monasteries were is where they themselves would have to make a living for communities that grew rapidly and grew large. Whatever the quality of the land, they would have to till it and enhance it and harvest it and live from it. All over Europe, monastics cleared the forests and put back into cultivation land that had been left barren and sterile by the barbarian multitudes that had allowed it to fall into ruin. Some groups of monastics, the Cistercians, even preferred to settle in wilderness areas where they cleared the ground and turned whole uninhabitable regions into some of Europe's most fertile farmlands or reforested valleys.

Around these large, stable communities, whose land was expanded yearly both by reclamation projects and the gifts of pious benefactors, grew up villages full of people for whom the monastery became employer, school, spiritual and social center. The monastery itself, then, became the local industry and social axis around which whole societies developed.

Property given to the monasteries, for instance, was seldom attached to the original land grant itself. Instead, the monastery fields, meadows, vineyards, forests and waters were spread across the continent. There were French monasteries with possessions in the eastern part of the empire, while the monastery of Fulda in Germany held land in Italy. By the year 1100, over two thousand communities were part of the Cluniac system alone, living, working, functioning, holding feudal renters, and producing in like ways all across Europe. As John Henry Newman wrote, Benedictines "were not dreaming sentimentalists, to fall in love with melancholy winds and purling rills and waterfalls and nodding groves...." No, these monks "could plough and reap, ...hedge and ditch, ...drain, ...lop, ...carpenter, ... thatch, ...make hurdles for their huts, ...make a road, ...divert or secure the streamlet's bed." And as they approached wilderness after wilderness this way, "the gloom of the forest departed...."

Most of all, each of the monasteries that lived under the Rule of Benedict operated with a vision of work and the land that marked the continent and its peoples for centuries.

The question is, then, What did these people learn from the monasteries that enabled them to salvage a dying continent from decay and misuse that might be good news to our own time?

The answer is that Benedictine monasticism is as much a way of seeing and working and living as it is a way of praying. It is a spiritual vision that affects a person's whole style of life.

The Rule of Benedict does not deal explicitly with the managing of property or the cultivation of land. What the Rule of Benedict is concerned with is the attitude that individuals take to everything in existence. As a result, this way of life has lasted for over 1,500 years and may well be as important to our own generation as it has been in times past.

Why? Because Benedict of Nursia's rule of life for monastics is not based on "taking dominion" over the earth as some readers of the Book of Genesis have emphasized. Benedict's theology of life is clearly based instead on the passage in Genesis that teaches that humanity was put in the Garden "to cultivate it and to care for it."

Benedict requires five qualities of the monastic that affect the way the monastic deals with the things of the earth: praise, humility, stewardship, manual labor and community, each of them designed to enable creation to go on creating.

Benedictine monasticism roots a person in a community of praise. Monastics are life-positive people whose attitudes are formed by the daily recitation of a psalmody that stresses the splendor of God in nature and the general goodness and connectedness of the cosmos. "Sun and moon, praise God," the monastic prays weekly. "Light and dark, wind and rain, praise God," the psalms go on. "Birds of the air and creatures of the sea, praise God." No gloom and doom religion here. In monastic spirituality, everything that is, is good and to be noticed and to be honored and to be reverenced. Nothing is expendable. Nothing is without a value of its own. Nothing is without purpose. Nothing is without beauty and quality and good.

For the holder of a monastic vision of life, then, to take from the land and not to replace it, to destroy it without reclaiming it, to have it without enhancing it is to violate the covenant of life. It was indeed a very monastic thing to replant the forests of Europe and to reclaim the swamps of France and to irrigate the fields of Germany in the Middle Ages. And it is a monastic gift, in an age that destroys with impunity, to recognize the value of everything, to recycle rather than to waste, to conserve energy rather than to pollute, to beautify rather than to distort an environment so that the whole world can come to praise.

Benedictine humility—the notion that we each occupy a place in the universe that is unique but not compelling, wonderful but not controlling—is an antidote to excess in anything and everything. In the Benedictine view of life, monastics are to have what they need and not a single thing more: a small room, the tools of the craft, a balanced diet, plain clothes, good books. The monastic is clearly to receive whatever is necessary. On the other hand, the monastic is to hoard nothing so that others, too, can have the goods of life. "Whenever new clothing is received, the old should be returned at once and stored in a wardrobe for the poor," the Rule reads. (RB:55) None of us, in other words, has an exclusive right to the fruits of creation.

It was humility and the sense of place that comes from it that led monastics of the Middle Ages to provide places of refuge for poor pilgrims and to house their noble novices in common spaces and simple cells alongside uneducated peasant monks and simple laboring types. It was humility that led monastics to care for the land rather than simply to live off of it.

In an age that preaches the gospel of rugged individualism and "free-market" capitalism, monastic spirituality is a gift thrown again at the feet of a society made poor for the sake of the oligarchy of the wealthy. Benedictine humility stands with simplicity in the face of greed, conspicuous consumption and the gorging of two-thirds of the resources of the world by one-third of the people of the world, Europeans and North Americans. The simple fact is that none of us can in conscience consume what belongs by human right to another.

Stewardship is a monastic mindset that fairly riddles the Rule. The monastic is to "care for the goods of the monastery as if they were the vessels of the altar." The abbot is reminded that he will be required "to give an account of his stewardship" of the monastery. "Let him recognize," he is told, "that his goal must be profit for the monastics, not preeminence for himself." The cellarer or manager of the monastery is told to steward the resources of the community "like a father," solicitous for "the sick, children, guests and the poor." (RB 31) Never does monastic life or any part of it exist only for itself and its own profit. What the Benedictine monastic does and has is always for the sake of the other.

In a world where control of resources, control of labor, control of profits, control of markets is the order of the day, monastic ecology calls for the cherishing of the entire planet and all of its peoples.

Manual labor, the actual shaping of our private worlds, is a hallmark of Benedictine monasticism. Every monastic, no matter how learned or how important, is, literally, to take life into their own hands by shoveling its mud and planting its seeds and carrying its boulders and digging its wells.

It was manual labor that made the monastic a co-creator of the universe where creation goes on creating daily. When you have washed a floor and fixed a chair and painted a wall and cleared an acre and cleaned a machine, the floor and the chair and the wall and the land and the machine become important to you. You have made yourself responsible for its life.

But responsibility for life is what the modern world has most lost. In a throwaway society, nothing is seen as having life. Things have simply a temporary usefulness. As a result, we have glutted our landfills with styrofoam cups, used once and used half and then discarded to lie unconsumed forever while we bury the human race in its own garbage.

Out of touch now with how long it takes to clean a polluted stream or grow a tree or dissipate a field of smog, we throw bottles overboard in our lakes and waste paper by the ream and allow three people in three cars to drive to the same place day after day after day. We have indeed come a long way from the fields and the kitchens of ages past and live now in cubicles of computers and machines, the effects of which have no meaning to us whatsoever. When a young man pushes the button to detonate a nuclear test, it is because he has lost a sense of the monastic vision of life that comes with working to preserve it with your own hands. When a young woman dumps the half-eaten casserole down a garbage disposal rather than eat leftovers, there is no sense of the monastic vision in her. When a family throws plastic cups out a car window, it is because they have lost a sense of the value of all things that comes with the manual labor that is essential to the monastic vision of the co-creation of life.

Finally, Benedictine monasticism is rooted in human community, stable, gifted, equal and needy. In the monastic community of the fifth century, when slavery was considered a natural part of the human condition, the members of the monastic community lived as equals, nobles and peasants, learned and illiterate, officials and members, side by side. Only respect for the amount of time spent in monastic life and the new kind of mentality that it formed in a society of violence and exploitation distinguished the place of one monastic from another.

Here in this world where no one was to be considered the servant or the lackey or the colony of the other, everyone had impartial claim on the goods of the community. Only the concept of "enoughness" regulated the distribution of goods in the monastic community. "Whoever needs less should thank God and not be distressed," the Rule instructs, "but whoever needs more should feel humble because of his weakness...." (RB: 34). In this society, that considered inner riches the wealth to be sought after, the notion of the accumulation of goods as a sign of character weakness was clear.

It is time to see the character weakness in our own patterns of conspicuous consumption and greedy capitalism. It is time to realize that the rest of the globe is not our backyard to dominate. It is our garden "to till and to keep."

It is precisely this monastic sense of praise, humility, stewardship, manual labor and community that taught Europe and fructified Europe and saved Western civilization. It is those things that we in our time lack now and to our peril.

Enlightenment for our age, too, as for the Sufi disciples of the tale, requires that we begin to see trees as trees and mountains as mountains again, but newly. We must begin to see the planet as something with a life of its own, holy and filled with the glory of God. It is not to be exploited by us or discarded by us or used by us for false and short-term profit. We must begin to see the sacredness of life itself, in all its forms, for all peoples of the earth. We must begin to understand that nature is not separate from us, it is basic to us. Its fate is our fate. Its future is our future. Its life is essential to our own.

If we can begin to see differently and to think differently and to live differently from generations before us then we will be able to grow enough crops to feed everyone. We will not only be able to draw water across deserts but we will be able to keep it clean and clear and healthful. We will have the paper we need at reasonable cost because we will have replaced the number of trees we need to make it. We will have the national security that comes when people are not threatened either by famine or futility. We will have a world where all people are paid just wages for the work of their hands. We will have a world where being part of an "underdeveloped" nation is a challenge, not a state of life, not a terminal disease, not an affliction without hope of cure.

Indeed, if we begin to see with monastic vision we may be able to save civilization once more. We will see all of life as good and refuse to dominate and diminish it. We will have the humility to know our place in the universe and respect, reclaim and revive the life around us. We will see ourselves as the stewards of the planet, not its owners, and we will pass it on to the next generation undamaged. We will work to shape a world full of beauty, full of possibility. We will build up the human community in such a way that there are no such things as "undeveloped" peoples.

Thomas Merton wrote once, "You have to take God and creatures all together and see God in creation and creation in God and

162

don't ever separate them. Then everything manifests God instead of hiding God or being in the way of God as an obstacle." It is the monastic vision that calls us to see the trees and mountains of our own day as part of the glory of God and to treat them accordingly.

Equality

A Woman's Place

There is an old Sufi story that may describe best the role of women in the Roman Catholic Church today.

In a Buddhist monastery in the Far East, the story tells, twenty monks and one nun, whose name was Eshun, were practicing meditation with a certain Zen master.

Eshun was very attractive and very holy and several of the monks fell secretly in love with her. One of them even wrote her a love letter, insisting upon a private meeting. But Eshun did not reply.

The following day the master gave a lecture to the group, and when it was over Eshun arose. Addressing the one who had written her, she said, "If you really love me so much, come and embrace me now."

The situation for women in the Roman Catholic Church today is, it seems, not all too different from Eshun's. Catholic women presumably are also loved, written glowingly about in fact, approached often in secret by clerics and bishops of all sorts who encourage their efforts in the woman's movement and doubt the value of the present practices of the church. Seldom, however, are women officially recognized and never, never are they formally embraced by the church in public: there are no women at the altar, no women in the Cardinalate, no women prefects of curial offices, no women expected in liturgical processions or as spiritual directors in seminaries or as the anointers of the dying whom they catechized.

We have reached the stage in the church obviously where women are to be heard but not seen. And that's the good news.

It has been much more in the character of the tradition for women not to be heard either. For centuries, and right up to our own time, women have been talked about only as sinners or as children, if they were talked about at all. The 1917 Code of Canon Law referred to women directly only once, for instance, and then only to say that "certain persons have a necessary legal domicile; a married woman the domicile of her husband, a minor the domicile of the parent; an insane person, that of his guardian." (c.93)

For the most part women were simply defined as morally threatening and intellectually inferior. Men, in fact, were cautioned to keep them at a distance, not out of concern for their own male weakness, but out of fear of the woman's wiles. John Chrysostom makes the inherent evil of women clear in his "On Priesthood." He writes:

"There are in the world a great many situations that weaken the conscientiousness of the soul. First and foremost of these is dealings with women. In his concern for the male sex, the superior may not forget the females, who need greater care precisely because of their ready inclination to sin. In this situation the evil enemy can find many ways to creep in secretly. For the eye of woman touches and disturbs our soul, and not only the eye of the unbridled woman, but that of the decent one as well." (VI, CH. 8.) He brooks no exception from the law.

"The whole sex is weak and flighty," he says. "What then, is there no salvation for them?" he asks. "Yes, there is," he says. "What kind? Salvation through children."(Ninth Homily on I Tim. 2:15)

As a result of teachings like these, normative in their content and universal in their application, laws were written to restrain women and books were written to guide them as good wives and mothers, the one arena acknowledged to be natural to them. Childbearing and childbearing alone became their role, not because childbearing was seen as woman's necessarily beautiful and spiritually creative contribution to the development of humanity but because women were seen as too bad for anything else, a totally carnal being in a world where flesh and spirit were at bitter conflict.

As a result, women were kept out of the sanctuary, out of the schools and out of the public domain. And all in the name of God. And for centuries and centuries.

The honest fact is, however, that things are not nearly as bad now as they were in my grandmother's time. The fact is, also, that things are not nearly as good now as they should be.

In my own lifetime, in the last fifty years in fact, there have been changes of monumental importance come wrapped in tiny, trivial packages. Both women and men, for instance, are permitted to sing in church choirs now, a task once reserved only to men and small boys with soprano voices.

The Churching Ceremony, which readmitted a woman to the church after childbirth in a manner reminiscent of the Jewish purification ceremony, has been abandoned and with it the feeling of banishment that came with doing the only thing that men said a woman was made for, giving birth.

Women are finally permitted to read the scriptures out loud and from inside the sanctuary of the church, a sign if there ever was one that they are a woman's scriptures, too.

Women can touch the vessels of the altar, a privilege once accorded to eleven-year-old altar boys but not to their mothers.

And in the wake of those breakthroughs, there are at least a few women chancellors and women department heads and women consultants to diocesan boards and women administrators of parishes and women judges on marriage tribunals.

There are a growing number of parishes who even encourage the presence of female altar servers and some make room, at least on special occasions, for women homilists—many of whom are better prepared theologically for the job than the regular parish priest. A few even change the male language of the hymns that trumpet "men's salvation" for all the women of the world to hear and to decide if this time the word really includes them or not.

The bishops themselves, in fact, have called for the elimination of sexist language in the reading of scripture to recognize that the Covenant is meant for women, too. We talk about "sons and daughters" now rather than simply the "sons" of God. Indeed there have been gains. Great gains.

Women now are routinely granted degrees in theology, the sole and private preserve of male clerics until the late '40s because it was a "sacred" subject and so out of the province of women.

The bishops have written a document, unpublished true, but written at least, which at long last and after millions of pious women submitted to the brutality of "the will of God for them" admits—declares indeed—that sexism is a sin and that wife-beating is immoral.

Make no doubt about it, there has been progress: minds have changed, attitudes are shifting, some behaviors are being corrected, expectations are high. The unthinkable, that women may be full human beings with all that implies theologically and socially, has become thinkable apparently.

To deny the progress of these times is not only to be unfair, it is to deny the very possibility of progress. If we forget where we have come from it may be impossible to maintain the energy it will take to get where we are going.

So, it is extremely important, I think, to remember aloud and always that once, and in this very generation in fact, we truly believed and passively accepted the notion that, since church music had been defined as a liturgical act, it was reserved for clerics and their male substitutes and that it was liturgically impossible, sacramentally deficient for women to sing in the church.

It is purposeful to remember that once not long ago we bowed quietly to the notion that no woman except, of course, a sacristan with mop in hand was allowed in the sanctuary because the sanctuary of God was a male domain where God did not want women, except as servants, of course.

It is functional to remember that though only some 40 years ago women were denied degrees in theology, that in the early 1990s women received 10% of the doctoral degrees, 25% of the bachelors degrees and 34% of the masters degrees in theology that were awarded in the United States alone.

In the light of such changes from the mundane to the momentous, it is essential to ask what there is now that we passively accept and docilely bear as God's will for women that is changeable, that must be changed, if the church is to be church.

The point is that because women have some rights now that they did not have before, it is easier to contend and clearer to see that they should have all of them. When the immutables became mutable, the church and the world may indeed have changed but they clearly did not end as some supposed and a lot of people have profited from the changing of them, men as well as women.

With the expectation that women, too, will be self-directed adults, we have men now who are liberated from the burden of playing God: to have to be all-knowing and all-powerful when a person needs and feels weak can lead either to tyranny or to breakdown. With admission to the adult world, we have women with higher self-esteem and less mental illness because they are finally being allowed to develop and encouraged to participate in the public dimensions of life. With the education of women, we have teachers of religion now who are grounded as well in theology as they are in piety. With the routine presence of women on church boards and planning committees, we have another whole dimension of spiritual and social life being expressed at the centers of the parishes. With the acknowledgment that women, too, have spiritual insights and theological creativity, we have the beginning of the expression of a feminine spirituality and a feminist theology that is both critique and call to traditional constructs. With the development of feminist exegesis, we have a richer reading of scripture and a freer expression of liturgy. With a church that is becoming both male and female—theologically, liturgically,

168

pastorally—we have the beginnings of a celebrating human family.

We are a richer people for it and that new richness must be recognized, admitted, and celebrated.

But there is a great deal that women do not have as yet, as well. Like Eshun, women get love but they get little respect. Women are made exceptions to in the church instead of the measure of its wholeness and authenticity. Indeed now, there is almost always one woman on every church committee, one woman on every theological panel, one woman on every parish staff. But there are seldom balanced numbers of them. They are tokens, in other words, and tokenism is not theological development. Tokenism is commitment to a theology of deviance.

The problem with tokenism is that it takes a few outsiders into the center of the system in order to keep the rest of the population out and make the system look good at the same time. The problem with tokenism is that nothing really changes. The system stays the same: the powerful are still powerful; the outsiders are still outsiders; the norm is still the norm. The tokens on the parish councils and episcopal committees become the window dressing on the religion, but not a clearly substantial and essential part of any diocese, any parish, any church enterprise, any theological deliberation. The new look is paraded and applauded but the old theology remains operational. It is men who bless them and shrive them and judge them and tell them what God wants of women since God, apparently, does not deign to deal with women directly, all the saints and mystics of the church to the contrary, all Marian theology aside.

It is men, after all, who make the exceptions that allow all the token women of the world to attend their meetings. There is no decree, no requirement, no right that is being honored. The world stays securely the same. It is men who make the rules and men who have the power to take them away.

Clearly, a great deal more will have to change before we will be able to tell with certainty that God decided to "make them in God's own image," and so "male and female God made them."

Some important dimensions are lacking, without which we

will be very unlikely to progress beyond the sterile, the safe and the secure in the question of the role of the women in the church. And never to the holy.

The spiritual concept of God must be reclaimed.

The continuing emphasis on God as Father rather than on God as Spirit, as Life, as Essence, as all Being is very subtly limiting of women and very clearly controlling of them. If God is male then males are, indeed, closer to God. Femaleness becomes the undivine other, the leftover, the unknown, the unholy, the addenda. And, of course, the subordinate. But even to hint at the possibility that the generation of life is an exclusively male prerogative by arguing that God must be seen as father because God is the generator of life is to participate in embarrassingly bad biology. It is, then, even worse theology. Heresy, perhaps.

Maleness, as a result, has become the new idolatry, the new golden calf which we worship in our churches and confirm in our social structures. Consequently, the feminine dimensions of God go unnoted and unknown in a world that has appropriated the warrior God to its militaristic self but has completely overlooked the birthing God who gives us all everything we need for life, if we will only distribute it.

We will certainly be what we worship. But we worship only half the reality of life. Of course God is a personal God. Of course God is father. But God is much more than that as the language of the church has always maintained. We have traditionally called God rock, fire, dove and lion. We must begin to ask ourselves, then, why we never, ever call God mother.

As long as our image of God remains so narrow, so will our experience of God in the world. So will our vision of church.

Sacramental theology must begin openly to challenge its inconsistencies and internal contradictions.

If baptism does indeed "make new creatures of us all," then why do only some of us get to grow to a full stature of this new creaturehood? If women are really equal in the image of God, then why are women denied sacramental access to God without the medium of a male? Why is it that we have wrenched the doc-

170

trine of "Incarnation" to the point that we prefer to believe that Jesus became male rather than that "the Word became flesh?"

If women are really "bone of my bone, flesh of my flesh," then they are surely equal if for no other reason than the DNA. Why, then, do we insist on the doctrine of complementarity rather than equality?

Why is it, in other words, that we say that women can get some graces, but not all graces? Why is it that women can receive grace, apparently, but never, ever dispense it?

The point is that our theologies of baptism, incarnation, grace, redemption and Eucharist are askew, at war with themselves, incompatible. The point is that if grace is not gender-specific, then God may have absolutely outrageous plans for women that man-made institutions have no right to obstruct.

We are to believe that the God who would choose a woman to turn God into the body and blood of Christ never wants a woman to do the same with bread.

It is not what sexism says about women that is sinful. It is what sexism says about God that is wrong. Sexism really implies that God is all powerful—except when it comes to women, at which point the God who could draw water from a rock and raise the dead to life is totally powerless to work as fully through a woman as through a man. Indeed, have no doubt about it: It is God who is being held hostage to sexism and, as a result, the world.

The images of women must change.

Once the image of God is twisted and the image of grace is warped, it is only a small step away from the ruination of the image of woman herself. She becomes body but not brain, functionary but not force, child but not adult, creature but not person.

We have defined woman as "mother" but we have not defined man as "father." We have called woman "helpmate," but we have not called man "partner." We have defined woman as irrational and man as rational, an arrogance in the wake of the human history of holocaust and nuclearisim and present technological warfare that boggles the mind. It is those very things, perhaps, that may prove the undoing of a people who have cut off half their human sensitivity.

It is time to realize that we need one another as persons, each-to-each a lesson, a call and a model; each-to-each servant and helpmate and friend.

Has the woman's movement failed? Why aren't the young as vigorous in their pursuit of the woman's movement as their mothers and grandmothers had apparently been? Have we wasted our time? Have we done the wrong things? Is the heritage of the woman's movement a broken church, a disoriented society?

I've spent a lot of time thinking about those questions. As a result I began to ask questions of my own. One day, for instance, I simply went from office to office and reading station to reading station in a small college library and asked other women, young and old, "Is your life any different because of the woman's movement? And, if so, how?" The answers were at least provocative if not astounding.

Older women were quick to respond. In the last 20 years, one said, there is "a different attitude toward women. There's greater respect for their intelligence," but, she added, "there's still inequality of salaries so I don't know how much of the respect is real yet."

The younger middle-aged woman beside her said, "Well, I'm not afraid of hitting them head-on now. If something's wrong, I don't take a back seat anymore. I was quiet but when you see other women standing up for their rights, then you can, too. I'm a single parent. If you don't stand up, you're left with nothing." Then she lowered her voice a bit. "But the woman's movement is very hard for men," she said. "We know now that we can do almost anything and men don't like that. Women have changed. They'll take power now."

One of the library assistants said, "We look at our children differently now. My daughters say, 'Mom, why didn't you play hockey when you were a child?' and I don't know how to tell them that we weren't allowed to do those things. No woman ran a marathon and if they did let us play games like basketball they wrote girls' rules because they said we couldn't run the full court like the boys did. And we believed them," she said with a touch of both wistfulness and anger in her voice.

The woman checking the book out at the counter was very thoughtful for a moment. "Well, lots has changed but we still fall into stereotypes. In some ways it has worked to our disadvantage. Now women have to deal with new expectations, old roles and triple the work."

"Oh, yes, my life is different as a result of the woman's movement," the secretary said. "Women get a lot more respect. They can go into different fields. They're taken seriously. And," she added with emphasis, "they can get out of bad situations." But then she thought for a moment. "There's just one thing," she said finally. "It's harder now for a woman to stay at home. In the first place, a family can't afford it. And now," she added, "the value of homemaking has just been lost."

It was the younger women, though, who left me with the most to consider. "What do I think about the woman's movement?" one of two young students said while she went right on filling out her registration forms. "Well, to tell you the truth I never really think about it at all. But if you ask, I think women are losing their femininity to it. I mean they're all so business oriented and they don't want to have children."

"The woman's movement hasn't helped me at all," one of the secretaries behind the office counter said. "It just raised all the prices after women began to work so now everybody has to work to make up the money we lost when men started losing jobs to women."

"Just wait a minute," the second of the students said. "Personal development is important to human growth for women as well as for men. I know that a lot of the message of the woman's movement has been lost because of the style of the messenger but we're forgetting something. Women have always worked. My mother worked. It's just that now I have choices that she never got. And it shouldn't be called the 'woman's movement' in the first place. Everyone is involved and benefiting from it. Women have helped men to grow. This is a human movement and we need it plenty."

"What would happen if we lost the woman's movement?" I asked. "Oh, you can't go back," the older woman said and gasped at the thought.

"I'd still be in bed sleeping," the secretary said, "and I'd have more money."

"We'd regain a family-oriented society and have time for our children," the first student said. "Society would be a lot better off."

The other women in the room, except for the secretary whose head was nodding, turned and looked at her. There was a moment of total silence and then the student added, with a giggle and a sigh. "But I don't know. I'd be awful bored staying home. You can only shop so much, you know."

In one conversation I had heard it all: woman as powerful, woman as respected, woman as victim, woman as troublemaker, woman as mother, woman as ornament, woman as person, woman so sure she'd arrived at that point of humanity that is self-directing, autonomous, free and valued that she doesn't even think of the woman's movement now. I knew instantly that the question was a central one and a complex one. The real truth lay surely in the fact that the woman's movement has both failed and succeeded and that sometimes it was hard to tell one dimension of it from the other.

What has the woman's movement really managed to do?

Part of the answer, of course, lies in determining where you want to start with the answer, at the suffragettes or at the publication of Betty Friedan's *The Feminine Mystique.* If we start with the suffragettes, of course, it is clear that we now have a female electorate in what had otherwise been a male republic for the 150 years prior to my grandmother's time.

If we start with Betty Friedan, on the other hand, we have a situation that may be more amazing perhaps than the gaining of the right to vote itself. Now we also have a female electorate that is strong enough and clear enough to be courted by politicians and analyzed by exit polls. There is a recognized woman's agenda and women candidates for public office and a woman's caucus in the Congress of the United States that monitors and promotes and writes and presses for legislation that is favorable to the concerns of women. In a culture historically more attuned to the problems of General Motors or the Pentagon or the savings and loan institutions of the country, it is no small thing to have someone notice legislation that discriminates against women or, worse perhaps, simply ignores the issues of child care or food stamps or medical assistance because the children, the poor, the elderly women of the world have no voice, no organization, no time for protest while they struggle in the lowest of low paying jobs to support the children of the men who abandoned or beat them.

The women's movement has forced academia to admit male and female students on equal terms rather than on the quota systems of the 1970s that required higher admissions criteria of young women than young men for far fewer available places. Girls have the right to full physical development programs now. They can compete in intercollegiate sports and have fully salaried coaches and team busses. But they don't, for the most part, get prime time television coverage. And they don't get high paying professional salaries no matter how good they are. Worse, we know that it isn't the idea of women working that is the problem. Women are definitely allowed to work the food stands at men's games for slave wages or cheerlead in scanty clothes for absolutely no pay at all. What is not permitted is that women's sports, too, become as respected and common as men's. The continuing question, of course, has to be, Why?

We have to ask why women are denied constitutional rights and education and property and freedom throughout the world and we must look to our theological concepts of God and creation and men for the answer.

We must ask why women work twice as many hours as men do in this country alone and ask what our churches teach about the role of women for an answer.

We must ask why women are paid only half as much as men for work that is every bit as difficult, every bit as important and

175

face what our churches maintain is the will of God for half the human race to understand the social situation.

The woman's movement has done much in society but most important of all, perhaps, the woman's movement has brought the theology of the church to a point of new development without which social structures will never change.

John XXIII in the encyclical "Pacem in Terris" called the shifting role of women one of "the signs of the times" along with the emergence of the Third World and the plight of the poor. And, good Pope John also writes in that document, that "those who discover that they have rights have the responsibility to claim them."

It is the claiming of those rights in the image of God, it is the development of a theology of humanity that will determine either the success of failure of the woman's movement. It may at the same time determine the future of the church as well.

The Sufi tell another story important, I think, to our own understanding of how meaningful the woman's movement is to the spiritual life of us all. This story tells that once upon a time a Holy One who lived as a hermit on the mountain was asked by a disciple, "Holy One, what is the Way?"

"What a fine mountain this is," the Holy One said in reply. "I am not asking you about the mountain," the disciple said, "I am asking you about the Way."

And the Holy One replied, "So long as you cannot go beyond the mountain, my friend, you cannot reach the Way."

The woman's movement raises the most important questions of life. It forces us to face and think about and deal with the nature of relationships, the nature of humanity and the nature of God. There can be no real holiness without it.

The implications are clear: If we do not go beyond this mountain, we cannot reach the Way.

It is time to realize that because we have not seen women as persons, full of grace, made in the image of God that we have a world governed by one-half of the human heart, understood by only one-half of the human mind, and grown to only half the stature of the human soul. We are a handicapped people and a handicapped church.

We have done quite well considering our affliction, but we are not well, we are not whole, we are not totally human yet.

Indeed, we too have loved Eshun secretly but we have failed to embrace her in public. And it shows. In both church and state.

Clearly we are missing the mountain.

Leadership

Fulfilling the Promise:
The Role of Leadership in the Church

There is probably no more elusive or more distressing concept in the history of human thought than the topic of leadership. Every major period in history has attempted to analyze it.

Plato dealt with the idea of the philosopher-king. Confucian thinkers evaluated leadership on its moral teachings. Plutarch dealt with the effect of age on public service. And contemporary social psychologists have splintered the idea into 130 separate definitions. It is no surprise, then, that the folklore of every people is full of ideas on leadership.

Ages ago, one sage, in fact, wrote: "When a million people follow you, ask yourself where you have gone wrong." And somewhere an apocryphal bishop is said to have lamented: "Wherever Jesus went there was a revolution; wherever I go they serve tea!"

And those homey little insights do indeed give light to the topic, but it's two ancient religious stories, though, that may best demonstrate the need for coming to grips with the nature of leadership in the church.

The first story is from the Hasidim: The Jews of a small town in Russia, the story recalls, were eagerly awaiting the arrival of the rabbi. Since this was such a rare event the townsfolk had spent a great deal of time preparing the important questions they were waiting to put to such a holy man. When the rabbi finally arrived and met with them in the town hall he, too, could sense the tension in the assembly as they froze in place to listen to his words. But, sensing the situation, the rabbi said nothing at all. He simply gazed into their eyes and began to hum a very haunting melody. Soon everyone there began to hum. He started to sing and they sang along with him. He swayed and danced in solemn, measured steps. And the congregation swayed and danced as well. Soon they were all so involved in the dance, so absorbed in its movements that they were lost to everything else on earth, completely centered on that moment, and, at the same time, completely lifted up beyond it, as well.

It was nearly an hour before the dance slowed down and came to a halt. Then the rabbi spoke the only words he pronounced that entire night. "I trust," he said, "that I have answered your questions?" And then he disappeared into the dark, not to be seen in that place again for years. But it was all right that he was gone because those people had learned that there was a great dance in life that they could dance themselves.

The second story is from the Sufi tales. Once upon a time the disciples said to the Holy One, "Tell us what you got from enlightenment. Did you become divine?" "No, not divine," the Holy One said. "Did you become a saint?" "Oh dear, no," the Holy One said. "Then what did you become?" the disciples asked. "I became awake," the Holy One said.

To enable people to become awake and involved, involved and awake may well be the greatest thing that leadership can do for anyone. The leadership questions for today, I think, are: What models of leadership do we have to draw from to awaken and involve the church? What kind of leadership do we need now in the church? And lastly, How shall we know authentic Christian leadership when we see it?

James Macgregor Burns, winner of the Pulitzer prize and national book award for his interdisciplinary study of leadership, defines four major types of transforming leadership. The leadership types that change society, he says, are intellectual leadership, reformist leadership, revolutionary leadership and heroic or charismatic leadership.

Each of these types, Burns argues, provides another dimension to the life of a group; each of them depends on circumstances; each of them is necessary if the group is to develop beyond the present and each of them is a specialized gift. Leadership, in other words, is a function of the community at large, not of one person. Leadership depends on a flow of special gifts which emerge at special times and leadership is an attitude of openness to be cultivated in everyone if a group is to thrive at all.

"You harm your own spiritual life if you make me your authority," the elder said to a starry-eyed disciple, "because by depending on me you refuse to see things for yourself."

Only power, you see, can be exercised in isolation. Leadership is a demonstration of the relationship between the leaders and the led, a situation where the needs of the led provide the goals of the leaders who then transform the world to meet those needs in one of four ways.

Intellectual leadership, Burns says, transforms society because it weighs practice against theory and theory against practice. It scrutinizes what is in the light of what must be. It is intellectual leadership that faces conflict in a society and seeks to interpret it. Intellectuals stand at the crossroads of human development and dare the questions.

Intellectuals look contention square in the eye and aim to face it down. Intellectuals raise the issues which plague us but perplex us. They set out consciously, for instance, to deal with questions of sexuality in a puritan culture and questions of war in a macho culture and questions of life in a bloody culture and questions of authority in a repressive culture. They set out to awaken us. The church that suppresses its thinkers and silences its theologians and cuts off its discussions will soon be a church without questions, without intellectuals, and without intellect.

In a world in transition, the church that sacrifices its Leonardo

Boffs and Charles Currans on the altar of authority prostitutes its leadership and will soon be a church without respect. Surely faith is strong enough for questions and certainly the living tradition can exist without traditionalists. Without intellectualism the mind of the church will die.

But that is not the model we have been given. Solomon was an intellectual who brought the chosen people to brave the central problems of the day, to think beyond past ideas, to broaden the scope of their lives. And we nourished intellectualism at the time of Vatican II. Can we possibly do less now and claim to lead the church in an age of more questions than answers? Indeed this is a critical period. If you and I are quiet now, it will take 50 years simply to legitimate the questions again, let alone to embrace the obvious answers.

Reformist leadership sets out to bring a whole community, a diverse community, to a state of change so that it can become again the gift to the world that once it was when it was fresh with meaning, splendid with purpose.

The problem for reformers, however, is that reform requires the cooperation and participation of every segment of the system, the commitment of all of its factions equally and individually, the concentration of all of its perspectives on one overriding goal, the exertion of all its leaders to lead in one direction. Reformers, Burns points out, must, therefore, deal with endless divisions within their own ranks. Reformers do well to step into the future on tiptoe. They are walking through minefields with snowshoes on. Reformers must work to bring involvement to the sectors and the edges to the center so that new light can fuel what has gone dim over time. But consciousness-raising is not the major problem of reform.

The major obstacle to reform is that reform demands changes in the very groups that must be counted upon to lead those changes. For instance, to reform liturgy it takes liturgists—the very people who may be most vested in its present structures—to reshape the rites of the past so that the people of this age, men and women alike, lay and cleric alike, can find a home in the heart of the church now.

To reform the church, then, we need chief liturgists themselves—we need bishops in other words—who will argue that women's feet, too, are fit matter for washing on Holy Thursday. To reform the clergy it will take clerics who are most privileged by clericalism to give it up so that they can finally give the church back to the people who really own it, the laity who carry its responsibilities but enjoy few of its rights.

To reform the ministries of the church it will take nuns, the very ones who are most comfortable with the institutions they have always had, to muster the kind of courage and spirituality it will take to shape new ministries, ministries that will raise to life this generation's poor blacks and poor Hispanics and poor women as they once brought to life in a protestant world whole generations of poor Germans and poor Italians and poor Irish and poor Slavs.

And to reform the role of the laity it will take the laity who have been conditioned into being consumers of the faith rather than channels of it to assert their own leadership role in the church, to take responsibility for the life of the church and to demand a hearing in the heart of the church as Canon 14 of "the fundamental law" challenges them to do when it speaks of "the rights of all the Christian faithful to receive assistance...especially the Word of God and the sacraments."

"People are led by the way they wish to follow," the Talmud teaches. It is time for us to learn the same. People get the leadership they demand.

To reform the church will require taking a curia that is used to being the center of the church and turning it into the servant of a church full of differences, full of needs.

The point is that any reform which is not led by the leaders of the culture to be reformed cannot possibly succeed. If Vatican II, in other words, is not accepted, it will not be the fault of the people. It will be because those entrusted with the completion of the council themselves resisted the call of the council and fanned division in the church rather than forging the alliances necessary to reform it.

If Vatican II fails it will be because the leaders of the church refused to lead. Vatican II will not die in the churches, it will die in the chanceries of the world. Reform requires a leadership that does not take sides, and does not pit one side against another: CUFF against Women's Ordination Conference, Opus Dei against Pax Christi, the vernacular Mass against the Tridentine Mass. A real reform leadership brings people together around a common hope, a pervasive commitment, a universal dream: the renewal and revitalization of the church.

At heart, you see, reform has nothing to do with the survival of the church; reform has to do with the survival of the gospel, a commodity far too rare to risk for the sake of bureaucracies, far too precious to spend on clerical litmus tests.

For that is not the model we have been given: Queen Esther was a reformer who risked her own life to guarantee life for her people. She measured the forces arrayed against the revitalization of the Jewish community and spoke the hard truth of common human needs, not division of the community and not the defeat of those who were different from the ruling elite. Let us have bishops named Esther who are willing to die so that the church might live, who care more for development than they do for authority.

In a church riven by differences as it was when the council of Jerusalem first reformed its very composition, let us again raise up Esthers everywhere.

Revolutionary leadership, Burns' third schema of transformation, is leadership that guides, with a powerful sense of mission and transcendent purpose, those cultural undercurrents that cannot possibly be undone under any circumstances. Revolutionary leadership is awake to the world around it and prepares a people to direct its reshaping, rather than to hunker down frightened and passive before the riptides and undertows of the present, yearning for a stagnant past.

Today the world around us is in a state of shuddering upheaval. Every institution known to humankind is in a process of redefinition: Education, government, marriage, science, ethics, economics, religion, religious life, church and human gender roles are all reeling from the findings of science and the impact of psychology and the emergence of global consciousness and the immediacy of communications and the implications of outer space. It is, without doubt, revolution time.

But revolution time is no time to choose authority over development. Revolution time is no time to choose past answers over new questions. Revolution time is no time to choose obedience over thinking. On the contrary, it is time to join the revolution. So that the tradition can be scuttled? No, no, my friends, so that the tradition can be saved. Godfrey Diekman, the great Benedictine liturgist, said once, "Tradition is not the stuff we pass on; tradition is the passing on of the stuff."

Well, we need now the passing on of guiding principles, not the passing on of vacuum-packed answers. We need a church that confronted by situations new to all of humankind will say "We don't know the answer to that right now, but we dearly honor the question." The fact is that white, western, medieval, and male certainties are dead; we need a respect for holy uncertainty now. We need a tolerance for the untried. We need a new worldview. We need a welcome of the spirit.

Human beings have lost control and God is back in charge again. We need now a leadership and a church that can live in ambiguity without apology and without fear—a leadership that cares more for the spirit than for the law, that cares more for the search than for the control it takes to maintain itself.

Surely it was a sense of search that directed the development of the peace pastoral and directed the passage of the pastoral on the economy and just as surely it was control, not a sense of search, that directed the pastoral on women in a world that requires more inclusion than privilege, more nurturing than wrenching, more of the feminist worldview than the macho mentality if we are ever again to be either whole or safe.

Indeed, it is revolution that is called for when the world as we knew it turns upside down without our permission. And it is a simpering, pathetic response, unworthy of the scriptures upon which it is based, that in times such as this we get authority rather than leadership, we get no to women preachers in the face of the Mary of the Magnificat, we get no to a Jesus who became flesh, not male, and we get no even to the discussion of priestly women and ordained family men while the people are starved for Eucharist in a sacramental church—and that in the face of Peter and his mother-in-law. And then they say no even to a God who is pure spirit in order to make maleness the new golden calf in the ecclesiastical desert.

That is not leadership and that is not the model we have been given for times such as these.

Moses was a revolutionary leader who saw the suffering and dissatisfaction of his people, who saw discrimination and deprivation and who, therefore, led them out of Egypt before they died from the disease of staying in a place long past life-giving for them.

Moses knew that it was time for revolutionary leadership, time to liberate a people from their oppressive past and their barren present in favor of the God who saves, despite the fact that he, too, had been part of that system himself. He , too, had grown up in it and made that no excuse for keeping it; he, too, had profited from it; and he, too, was protected by it and respected because of it. And he did it despite the fact that the band he led was nobodies with nobody to care for them.

The women of the church and the poor of the church and the lay people of the church and the dispersed of the church are leading a revolution to give the church back to the nobodies of today's church, too. And that is leadership. For the sake of the church may the leadership someday join it. Surely, we must not take another four hundred years to admit the content of this era's revolution in the church as we did the one before it.

Finally, Burns describes a final category of leaders: The heroic or charismatic who through the power of their presence and the force of their ideas give fire to light. What the intellectuals think about, what the reformers plan for, what the revolutionaries demand, heroic leaders embody. Heroic leaders, Burns teaches, provide a symbolic solution to a real conflict.

They themselves become what the crisis demands—profound peacemakers, strong women, men of courage and truth. They begin to live differently than the world has taught them to live. They are the carriers of our highest aspirations who refuse to bow down to the limits society would impose on them. They live into our dreams right before our eyes. They combine vision and life. They make the possible real. We look at them and our faltering faith becomes hope again.

They are the people to whom Albert Schweitzer referred when he wrote, "Sometimes our own light goes out, but it is blown again into flame by an encounter with another human being. Each of us owes the deepest thanks to those who rekindled this light."

They are the Tom Gumbletons who live peace and the Rembert Weaklands who live truth and the Raymond Luckers who live the questions and the Michael Kenneys who live courage. They are the Matthew Clarks and Frank Murphys who live for a gender-free church. They are the Raymond Hunthausens and Oscar Romeros who have died a hundred deaths for truth. They are all the bishops of this country who have jeopardized their place in the system for the sake of the gospel.

They are the women of the Women's Ordination Conference and the ministers of Priests for Equality and the lay people from Call to Action and the peacemakers of Pax Christi. They are the Martin Luther King, Jrs. and Thomas Mertons and Dorothy Days, the Dan Berrigans and Dietrich Bonhoeffers, the Rosemary Reuthers and Thea Bowmans and Marjorie Tuites and Mary Luke Tobins whose leadership has never been made official, but who are leaders nevertheless. They are the ones who follow in the footsteps of all those legions of figures who have reshaped the mind of the church before us: Benedict and Francis and Ignatius and Teresa of Avila and Catherine of Siena and Mary Ward.

They are the ones who never held great authority but who always held great influence because no amount of power and no degree of authority can ever substitute for the eternal echoes of the persuasive ring of divine truth in the human heart. Heroic, charismatic leaders do not caution caution. They do not turn the church into a bureaucracy bent on protecting the system from the spirit for that is not the model we have been given.

The prophetess, judge and leader Deborah was a married lay woman who sat daily under a royal palm giving people in darkness a taste of light and insights into the mind of God. In the face of national oppression she called the official leaders of the people to accountability and rallied a veritably defenseless Israel against Sisera's 900 iron chariots where, on the strength of her courage and charisma, they routed them.

She spoke out against oppression by the state and took her place at the head of the people to call the community back to the vision of God when it had strayed into the voiceless swamp of conformity and quiet acquiescence to the evils of the time. Deborah stood up to raw power and it crumbled at her feet and, through her, an Israel in decline was saved—by the instrumentation of a woman.

And Deborah, heroic leader, unofficial leader, calls each of us yet to be the same. It is we now who must sound the alarm of justice in a world where the new industrial slavery engorges the west at the expense of the east and bloats the north at the price of the future of the south; it is we now who must provoke the indifferent wealthy to see suffering in the midst of their affluence.

It is we now who must call the church to realize that in a patriarchal world it was God who ordained Deborah to ministry and it is God—now and here—who is raising up Deborahs again to call back to the gospel a church whose religion is religion; and whose leadership is clerical rather than ecclesial. It is we now, Deborah's descendants all, who must call the institutional leadership today whose predecessors once led the church to accept freedom of conscience and the pluralistic state and Vatican II to have the courage to lead this time against the sin of sexism in a world imperiled at every level by the institutionalization of the male model of life.

Indeed, Solomon calls the church to intellectual leadership

and Esther calls the church to reformist leadership and Moses calls the church to revolutionary leadership and Deborah calls the church to heroic leadership. And church history itself confirms the role of each gift in every major period. Solomon and Esther and Moses and Deborah, the thinkers and leaders and saints before us, in other words, are calling us to transform our world.

But how shall we know true church leadership when we see it? And how shall we ourselves in our time go about so great a task? The church is very clear about the answer.

Most poignant of all the prayers of the church perhaps, Advent's O Antiphons are among the most ancient elements of the advent liturgy. They are Christmas week's long, last wail of waiting for deliverance, for redemption, for leadership out of darkness. Most of all, these prayers describe quite clearly the type of leadership that marks the coming of the reign of God.

The O Anthipons are the cry of the church that Christ, for whom we wait, will this time be born in us. The O Anthipons present, I believe, the Christian model of leadership against which all church leaders must be measured and all church leadership must be evaluated, whatever its form: intellectual, reform, revolutionary or heroic.

The O Anthipons are unmistakably clear about the type of direction which must mark the Christian community. They describe seven qualities that are the measure of our merit: wisdom, strength, openness, patience, courage, justice and inclusiveness. The prayers are clear and our need for them is great.

Come, *O Wisdom* from on high, the church teaches us to pray and, God knows, the church needs wisdom now. Do not be fooled. Knowledge and wisdom are not the same thing. Knowledge we have aplenty—knowledge of canon law, and knowledge of church history, and knowledge of the various heresies and knowledge of the issues of the time. But what we need is wisdom enough to scrutinize life through the eyes of God. We need leadership with wisdom enough to begin to look at what is in front of us and ask what God sees in what we are not seeing. We need church leadership with wisdom enough to see what sexism is doing to men as well as to women, to the world as well as to the family, to the integrity of the church as well as to the resources of the state.

Indeed, it is wisdom, not knowledge, that this smart but macho world needs in its leaders now.

Come, *O God of Strength*, the O Antiphons pray but strength is a rare commodity. We like power, of course, and we're very good at it. As a culture we exterminate Iraqis and as a church we limit leadership to a few and expect compliance from everybody else. But strength is what God asked of Moses, not power. And it takes strength to give up power.

It will take strength to begin to see the laity as theologically enlightened rather than theologically illiterate. It will take strength to give up political prestige for prophetic presence in this society. It will take strength to become a church of grubby locust-eating changers in a world full of business suits.

Come, *O Flower of Jesse's Stem*, we pray when we pray for the leadership we really want. But who in heaven's name was Jesse? Jesse was a nobody. At least nobody I know knows him. Everybody knows Abraham, yes, Noah, yes. Samuel, maybe. But Jesse?

Historically speaking, Jesse is just a name in Jesus' genealogy, and an obscure one at that. But Jesse was the forebear of David, the one from whose line would come the messiah. Jesse was the unknown one, the one who began the great work whose end he would not see. Jesse had courageous faith. Jesse was the one who was able both to believe and to wait. To begin without knowing the end, to do what needed to be done, without being guaranteed its value.

We need leaders like Jesse now. We need leaders who will sow the seeds of new life and not grow silent in the waiting if life in all its forms is late in coming to the church. We need Jesses in the church now at a time when all the lay advisors and religious personnel and women department heads are being erased in dioceses. Who will begin once more to question institutional elitism so that the church of the "people of God" can someday at last become more reality than promise?

We need Jesses to go on insisting on Eucharist in a system

that is opting for maleness over sacramentalism in a sacramental church while the celibate, male priesthood declines with each passing day. Whatever the future needs we, like Jesse, must begin ourselves and begin now. And we must begin it with patience and with faith or our energies will flag and our best hopes will die.

Come, *O Key of David,* the church has us pray in our desire for leadership. It is a searing cry for the kind of direction that will open doors and break down barriers. We need a church that is solidly on the side of the poor, that preaches its social encyclicals from its pulpits and models them in its parishes, and stands for peace for everyone, not national privilege, around the world.

Come, *O Radiant Dawn,* we sing as we wait for the leader of leaders. Come, sun of justice, we plead. But it is not "the dawn of humankind," it is not justice, that comes when church leaders side with fascism in Haiti, and nuclearism in the United States, and military oppression in Nicaragua, and the barbaric destruction of Muslims in wars for oil. It is not justice when the church that decries apartheid when it is practiced by politicians theologizes it when it's practiced in parishes. We need a church that is just in itself so that its calls for justice carry the weight of gold in a world where other leadership has gone morally bankrupt.

We sing Come, *O God of All the Earth,* as we wait for the one who will end the anguished waiting of people everywhere. We need a church that embraces the world, that does not obstruct ecumenism with churches that see God's way with women differently as once they saw the worth of relics and the role of saints and the use of scripture and the place of conscience differently than we did and, so, finally converted us, too, because of it.

Finally, *O Come, O Come, Emmanuel* we pray as we wait for the leadership the world needs. "Come," we beg the One who is God of all, of everyone, the One who leaves no one out. "Come to us," we beg of the One who bends over female corpses and breathes life into them. "Come," we wail to the One who cures those crippled by lack of care in our systems and who, as a result, "have not stood upright" for years in our society. Come and be the bishops who take in our gay and lesbian brothers and sisters, come and inspire our parishes to open their doors to our divorced and separated families, come and fill our teachers with more concern for the gospel than for the rules. Come to us and change hearts, starting with our own so that the leadership we give will make us more a recklessly loving church than a well-ordered male institution.

Indeed the church needs leadership now that challenges, reforms, revitalizes and reminds the world in its own body that life as we know it, with its withering poverty, its destruction for profit, its exploitation and oppression of peoples can be different.

But this leadership must depend on wisdom, not knowledge alone; on strength, not power; on openness to new ideas, not control; on patient faith, not unyielding insistence; on courage, not fear of risk; on justice, not intractable authority and false or-der; on embracing inclusion, not elitism. Indeed, the O Antiphons are very clear about the nature of leadership. Let no one think otherwise.

An ancient people tell the story of a prophet who ran through the town with a flaming torch. "Prophet, where are you going with that torch?" the people called. "To burn the temple down," the prophet shouted back. "But why would you ever do anything like that?" the people cried. And the prophet answered as he ran, "So that you will learn as a people to pay less attention to your temples and more attention to our God." The needs are clear: May God raise up among us a leadership that will lead us in a dance we can do for ourselves; may God give us always leaders awake to the spirit in all of us; and may God make of all of us leaders less centered on the preservation of the institution than we are on the preservation of the gospel in our time.

And may God raise up among us a leadership more centered on the gospel than it is on the church. So that, please God, we may finally come, priests and people alike, to recognize and not revile, to support and not suppress the Solomons and the Esthers, the Moses and the Deborahs who are among us still, so that the fulfillment of the promise can surely come even here. Even now.

Acknowledgements

Benetvision gratefully acknowledges the following publications in which portions of this anthology previously appeared: "There Just Aren't Any Just Wars Anymore" appeared in *Salt*, May 1992; "Contemplation, Everyone?" was an interview published in *Praying Magazine*, January-February 1991; "The Justice Lessons Jesus Grew Up On" was published in *Salt*, September 1990; "Sins of the '90s: The Lost Sabbath" appeared in London's *The Tablet*, March 1997; "Why I Stay" was published in *Lutheran Woman Today*, October 1996; "The Bishop Who Said Sorry" was printed in London's *The Tablet*, January 1997; "Monastic Prayer: Unchanging Change" appeared in *Religious Life Review*, September/October 1998; "Icons, Rebels, Stars and Saints: Holiness in the Catholic Tradition" was published in the SIDIC (Service International de Documentation Judéo-Chrétienne) bulletin, July 1997; "Work: My Share of the Life of God" appeared in *Liguorian*, September 1993; "Simplicity of Life" also appeared in *Liguorian*, February 1995; "A Spirituality for the Long Haul" was published in *Compass: A Jesuit Journal*, June 1992; "Monasticism: An Ancient Answer to Modern Problems" was published as Chapter 5, "Monasticism" by Joan Chittister in *Christianity and Ecology*, edited by E. Breuilly and M. Palmer © The Continuum International Publishing Group. Reprinted with the permission of the publisher; "A Woman's Place" appeared in the *Notre Dame Magazine*, Winter 1991-92.

The following articles were given as speeches: "Discipleship for a Priestly People in a Priestless Period," a presentation given at the Women's Ordination Worldwide 1st International Conference in Dublin, Ireland, June 2001; "Both Roots and Wings: Moving the Vatican II Church Into a New Millennium," the concluding address at the three 2001 Call to Action National Conferences held in Los Angeles, Philadelphia and Chicago; "Thomas Merton: Seeder of Radical Action and the Enlightened Heart," the Guilfoil Memorial Lecture given in Kansas City, MO, February 2001; "Liturgy: To Comfort or Liberate," a presentation given at the Pastoral Musicians National Conference, Cincinnati, OH, October 1995; "Empowerment and Spirituality," a lecture given at the Future of the American Church Conference, Washington, DC,

September 1989; "Jesus at the Healing Pool of Bethsaida: A Model of Contemporary Ministry," a presentation given in St. Paul, MN, January 1990; "Fulfilling the Promise: The Role of Leadership in the Church," a presentation given at the Future of the American Church Conference in Washington, DC, September 1992.

Some of the writings were slightly edited for this anthology.